GAME DAY
PENN STATE FOOTBALL

GAME DAY
PENN STATE FOOTBALL

*The Greatest Games, Players, Coaches and Teams
in the Glorious Tradition of Nittany Lion Football*

TRIUMPH
BOOKS

Athlon® Sports™
AMERICA'S PREMIER SPORTS ANNUALS

Library of Congress Control Number: 2007900792

This book is available in quantity at special discounts for your group or organization. For further information, contact:

Triumph Books
542 South Dearborn Street
Suite 750
Chicago, Illinois 60605
(312) 939-3330
Fax (312) 663-3557

CONTRIBUTING WRITER: Matt Herb

EDITOR: Rob Doster

PHOTO EDITOR: Tim Clark
ASSISTANT PHOTO EDITOR: Danny Murphy

DESIGN: Eileen Wagner
PRODUCTION: Patricia Frey

PHOTO CREDITS: Athlon Sports Archive, AP/Wide World Photos, Penn State University Archives, Christopher Weddle (Nittany Lion Shrine)

Printed in China

ISBN-13: 978-1-60078-014-1
ISBN-10: 1-60078-014-1

Contents

As he's done countless times over his 40-plus years at the helm, Joe Paterno leads his Nittany Lions into battle at Beaver Stadium.

Foreword

by D.J. Dozier

If there is any one thing that symbolizes Penn State football, it is the plain blue and white uniforms that players have been wearing for more than 100 years. Today's football fans know who we are as soon as we step on the field. But our uniforms not only identify us as a team, they also tell a lot about who we are as individuals.

Like our uniforms, we are not fancy and we are not flamboyant. We have a strong work ethic and a strong sense of character. We have grit and we have that "never give up" attitude. We place our team and our teammates first.

Sure, Penn State has had its share of players who were more, let's say, "off the wall" than the rest of us. We had a couple on our undefeated national championship team in 1986. I can still remember linebacker Trey Bauer always having a few extra words to say to an opposing player after making a ferocious tackle, and he would occasionally find himself in Coach Paterno's dog house. But he knew how to get the job done on the field. In the end, Trey was no different than the rest of us on that team. He was a team player first, not an individualist.

We didn't get this way on our own. Joe Paterno set the standard, not just for our team, but for all the teams he coached in the last 40 years. Now, I know Penn State had a football tradition before Joe, and many of those coaches and players before him are in the College Football Hall of Fame. But Joe took the program to a new level. Today, his name is synonymous with Penn State football and rightly so, because he set a new standard.

It's a standard of excellence. If you want to be there, if you want to play and become a major contributor, you too must meet the standard, whether it means going to class or dressing properly or, most importantly, being on time. Any time you are coached and led by someone with such a precise and high standard, you can either abide by it or rebel against it. One of the reasons we were successful as a team in 1985 and 1986 is that a majority of us abided by the standard. We saw the bar that Joe set. We went after it with reckless abandon, and, obviously, we attained the coveted prize. Sometimes it seemed unattainable and it took us some time to get there. But we had enough character, enough instruction, and enough talent and ability to get where Joe was trying to take us.

There have been other great teams at Penn State, but the 1986 team that upset Miami in the Fiesta Bowl and won the national championship is the epitome of what a team really is. The bulk of the starters from the 1986 team entered Penn State in 1982 and 1983, and we were a team that not only had talent, but we were a close knit group. There's a photo from that year that some of the players, like our defensive end Bob White who's back working for Penn State, now have in their offices. It shows the defensive linemen holding hands. That photo is a great reflection of the closeness of the team in 1986. We stuck together through adversity and some tough times, and knew how to "keep our cool," set goals to get out of those tough times, and fight to get to a point where we were playing for the national championship.

It started long before that great night in Phoenix. I remember as a (true) freshman in 1983 how we started off losing our first three games, and Joe told us in the meeting room, "Hey guys, our backs are against the wall and we have a decision to make. We can either lie down or we can come out fighting." At that point the team came together, and if there is anything we knew at Penn State, we knew how to come together and play as one unit. We did not lose another regular season game and went on to beat Washington in the Aloha Bowl.

We stumbled in 1984, but that set the stage for 1985, when we went undefeated and became the number one team in the country, but lost the national championship to Oklahoma in the Orange Bowl. Yet, that defeat led us to the ultimate victory. The greatest victory sometimes comes out of the greatest defeat. After losing to Oklahoma, the seniors that could have left and gone on to the pros—like Shane Conlan and Don Graham—made a decision right there in the locker room to come back. From that night in the Orange Bowl stadium we immediately began to think of what was going to happen 365 days later. It was the moment that defined the character and commitment of our team. The group that came here in 1982 and 1983 had the privilege of playing together for three years with the finality of winning the championship in 1986.

We're still a close team and it's been slightly more than 20 years since we played together. But nowadays when I think of that team, I think mostly of Steve Smith, our starting fullback who did a lot of blocking that helped me become an All-American. Steve had a successful NFL career with the Oakland Raiders and the Seattle Seahawks and after retiring went into private business. But he is currently battling ALS, amyotrophic lateral sclerosis, which may be better known as Lou Gehrig's disease. He's fighting for his life. As a team, we're trying to help Steve and his family by not only being there to support them emotionally but with fundraising projects to cover some of their medical expenses. I know that if I or another teammate was in the same situation, someone on that team or a group of guys would rally to help one of us as well. And that's a reflection of who we are.

I am sure there are other Penn State teams that have had a similar rapport. I never saw them play but I've heard stories about the undefeated team of 1947 and those great defensive teams Joe had in 1968 and 1969. Some of the guys I played with also were on the national championship team of 1982, and I think the undefeated 1994 team, with guys like Ki-Jana Carter and Kerry Collins, were a lot like us. I would say the same of that 2005 team led by Michael Robinson.

Just like our group, those players have gone on to be successful after football. Some are businessmen. Some are on Wall Street. Some are lawyers. And some are teachers and ministers. We all wore those plain blue and white uniforms, and we wore them proudly. That's what Penn State football is all about and I am glad I have been part of it.

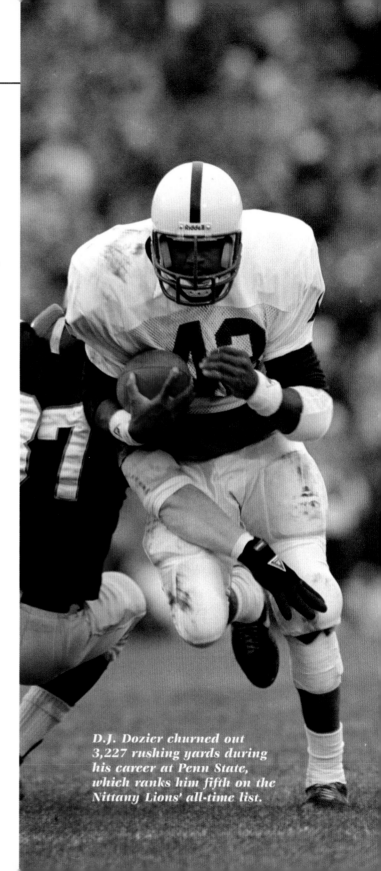

D.J. Dozier churned out 3,227 rushing yards during his career at Penn State, which ranks him fifth on the Nittany Lions' all-time list.

Introduction

The images are unforgettable and too numerous to count.

Joe Paterno, stalking the sidelines in his black shoes and white socks, peering through those distinctive dark-framed glasses as his teams define college football excellence. Those classically simple uniforms that underscore the Nittany Lions' team-first identity. John Cappelletti, moving a nation to tears with the most memorable Heisman acceptance speech in history. A packed Beaver Stadium, 107,000 strong, giving full-throated support to the blue and white. National championships won; legends created.

We're distilling the pageantry and drama of Penn State football into the pages that follow. It's a daunting task. Few college football programs in the country inspire the loyalty and passion that the Nittany Lion football program exacts from its fans—and with good reason.

The numbers alone are impressive: two national championships. An amazing five perfect seasons since 1968, the most in the nation over that span. The best bowl winning percentage in college football. Sixteen Nittany Lions in the College Football Hall of Fame.

But numbers alone don't do justice to the greatness of Penn State football. The Nittany Lion program stands for something deeper, a true appreciation for doing things the right way, for upholding the ideals of college athletics—and winning in the process.

Through the words and images we present, you'll get a taste of what Penn State football is all about. Decades have passed since players first donned the blue and white, but one thing hasn't changed: Penn State football is an unmatched tradition, a legacy of greatness, a way of life in the Keystone State.

Lion legend Bobby Engram (No. 10) celebrates another big play.

The Greatest Players

Penn State is all about the team. Players are supposed to check their egos at the door and devote themselves to a higher purpose. In ways big and small, the culture at Penn State reflects the coaching staff's team-first theme. This is a school that doesn't put names on the backs of its jerseys, a school that regards helmet numbers as garish displays of egotism run amok, a school that doesn't allow true freshmen to appear in the media guide. Joe Paterno likes it that way.

But there is an undercurrent of hero worship at Penn State. More than an undercurrent, actually. Attend a game at Beaver Stadium and you'll see thousands of fans with replica jerseys on their backs, all of them bearing the numbers of past or current favorites. The Nittany Lions have produced their share of All-Americans and Hall of Famers, and university officials, for all their emphasis on team welfare over individual acclaim, can't help but trumpet the occasional player or two. Or three.

The following overview isn't comprehensive, but it does highlight some of the best players in school history. Rest assured, Penn State fans know these names, even if they don't appear anywhere in embroidered letters.

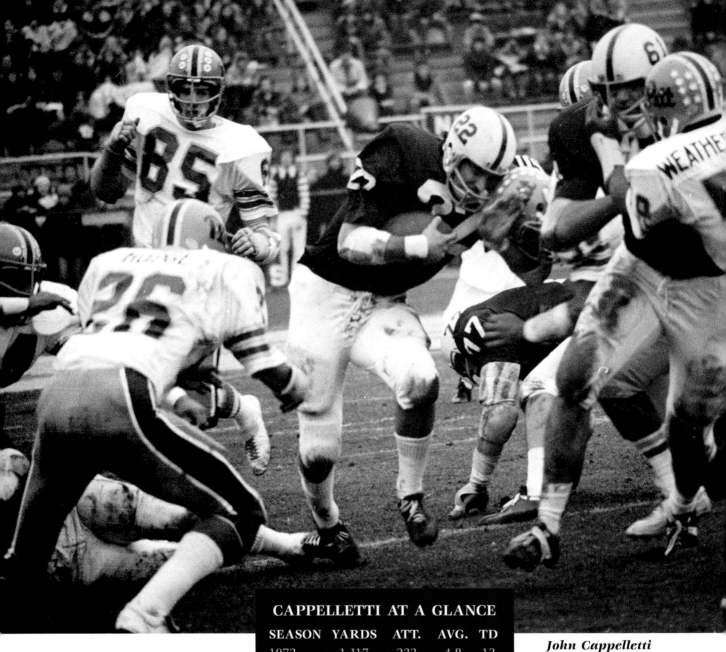

CAPPELLETTI AT A GLANCE

SEASON	YARDS	ATT.	AVG.	TD
1972	1,117	233	4.8	12
1973	1,522	286	5.3	17
Career	2,639	519	5.1	29

- Co-captain in 1973
- 13 career 100-yard rushing games
- Rushed for a career-high 220 yards on a Penn State-record 41 carries vs. NC State in 1973
- Lions posted 22–2 record with Cappelletti as the featured back

John Cappelletti

THE HEISMAN TROPHY WINNER

1973
John Cappelletti
Running Back
6'1", 225
Upper Darby, Pennsylvania

There have been better tailbacks to play at Penn State during the Paterno era. Faster. Bigger. More elusive. But none of those players ever won college football's most prestigious individual honor. And for all their on-the-field exploits, none of them ever touched the Penn State community—and the nation—quite the way Cappelletti did when he stood before the Downtown Athletic Club on the night of his enshrinement and dedicated the Heisman Trophy to his kid brother Joey, who was dying of leukemia.

Who was John Cappelletti? A lot of college football fans were probably asking themselves that question as late as 1972. He had been a star at Monsignor Bonner High School in suburban Philadelphia, but after two seasons at Penn State, he was hardly a familiar running back. In fact, he wasn't a running back at all. Cappelletti played in the secondary his freshman and sophomore years and also returned punts as a sophomore.

It wasn't until his junior season that he really took off. After they moved him to offense, Penn State's coaches quickly discovered that opponents had no answer for his formidable power and deceptive speed. Cappelletti rushed for 1,117 yards that year, and it turned out to be only a prelude to bigger and better things. As a senior, he was little short of unstoppable, finishing with 1,522 yards, 17 touchdowns and an average of 5.3 yards per carry. His yardage total is the fourth-best single-season mark in school history.

Like so many great running backs, Cappelletti got better with each carry. Late in the 1973 season, he surpassed 200 yards rushing in consecutive games against Maryland, North Carolina State and Ohio. Heisman buzz had steadily been building, but those three performances put him over the top. The trophy was his.

At the Heisman ceremony, Cappelletti got up to speak and soon found himself overcome. Joey was in the audience that night, along with a roomful of dignitaries that included Vice President Gerald Ford. No one knew what Cappelletti was about to say. He hadn't told anyone, not even fellow Penn State captain Mark Markovich, his roommate in Manhattan.

"A lot of people think I go through a lot on Saturdays, getting bumps and bruises," Cappelletti said, his voice quivering. "But for me, it's only on Saturdays and only in the fall. For Joey, it's all year round and it's a never-ending battle. The Heisman Trophy is more than mine because he's been a great inspiration to me. If I can dedicate this trophy to him tonight and give him a couple of days of happiness, it would mean everything."

Cappelletti's speech—if it could be called that—left onlookers in tears. The story captivated the nation and was soon made into a book and later a TV movie called "Something for Joey" starring Marc Singer as the young Penn State tailback. The movie aired in 1977, a year after Joey's death.

Cappelletti went on to play 10 seasons in the NFL with the Rams and Chargers. He retired after the 1983 season and got into the real estate business in Southern California. Now a father of four, he still gets letters from people who were in their teens when they first heard about his speech or saw "Something for Joey" on video. "It really hasn't subsided in 30 years," he told *USA Today* in 2003. "I don't think it will as long as there are people who identify with it."

One of these years, another player will likely join Cappelletti—or "Cappy" as he is known to fans—in the pantheon of Penn State Heisman Trophy winners. Other players have come achingly close to claiming the award. Rich Lucas, Chuck Fusina and Ki-Jana Carter all finished second in the balloting, while Larry Johnson was third after becoming the first Big Ten running back to surpass 2,000 yards rushing in a season.

But no matter when it finally happens, it's unlikely Penn State's next Heisman winner will touch the college football world quite the way John Cappelletti did on a December night in 1973.

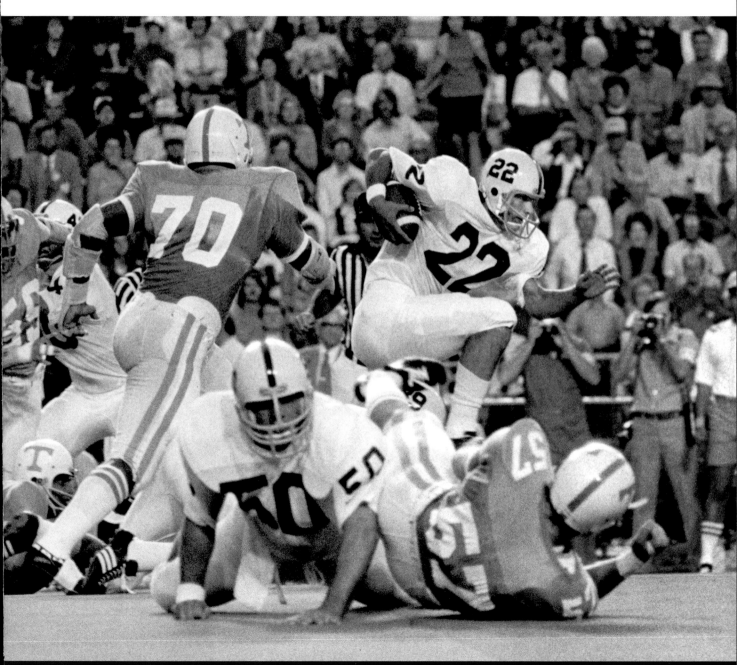

John Cappelletti churns out yardage against a vaunted Tennessee defense.

Dennis Onkotz

LINEBACKER U.

The origin of Penn State's celebrated nickname has been lost in the sweep of history. Was it a broadcaster who first referred to Joe Paterno's program as "Linebacker U."? Was it a writer? A coach? An historian? We'll probably never know. But there's a certain inevitability to it that renders its beginnings irrelevant. Penn State has produced some magnificent linebackers through the years. Let's leave it at that.

The first great Penn State linebacker predated Paterno's appointment as head coach. He was **Dan Radakovich**, a two-way star on Rip Engle's teams of the mid-1950s. Nicknamed "Bad Rad" for his famous mean streak, Radakovich had a huge impact on the school's emergence as Linebacker U. Not only did he turn the Nittany Lions' defense into an intimidating force with his fierce hitting, but he also became an assistant coach in the 1960s and taught the first generation of Paterno-era linebackers to play just like he did. They could hardly have had a better teacher.

One of the best of that formidable bunch was **Dennis Onkotz**. A two-time All-American and a driven student as well—he carried a 3.5 GPA in biophysics and was known to attend class on Saturday mornings before games—Onkotz was among the most versatile players in school history. He was so versatile that it's hard to believe there was only one of him. Onkotz had an uncanny nose for the ball, as exemplified by his 287 career tackles and 11 interceptions.

In addition, he returned punts, averaging 13.2 yards on 47 attempts. On the field or off, there was little this great student-athlete couldn't do.

Onkotz seemed destined for a great pro career, but it wasn't meant to be. Picked by the Jets in the third round of the 1970 draft, he had to give up football after his leg was badly broken during his rookie season. He was inducted into the College Football Hall of Fame in 1995.

During the last two years of his Penn State career, Onkotz lined up alongside a player some consider to be the best ever to play for Paterno: future Pro Football Hall of Famer **Jack Ham**.

During his collegiate career, Ham proved to be everything a linebacker is supposed to be—fast, aggressive, fearless. His development was miraculous, and his legend only grew when fans discovered just how unlikely a success story he really was.

Ham had been a late bloomer. Indeed, had he bloomed any later, he might never have played football for Penn State. The Nittany Lions didn't want anything to do with him when he came out of high school, and their disinterest was perfectly understandable. He had been a pedestrian offensive guard at Bishop McCort High in Johnstown, Pa., rising no higher than the second team.

It was only after a year of prep school that the Lions agreed to sign Ham. On the advice of defensive tackle Steve Smear, a

Greg Buttle (No. 67)

Jack Ham
(No. 33)

teammate of Ham's at Bishop McCort, the coaches gave him their last available scholarship. They would not regret the decision.

Once on campus, the 6'3", 212-pound Ham flourished. Paterno wasted no time getting him onto the field, and he proved the coach's faith well-founded, excelling as a sophomore in 1968 with three blocked punts. Ham went on to make 251 tackles at Penn State. He won consensus All-America notice as a senior and put himself in position to be taken in the second round of the 1971 NFL draft by a team that, unbeknownst to anyone at the time, was on the cusp of a dynastic reign over the NFL.

The once-unheralded linebacker became an eight-time Pro Bowler and won four Super Bowls with the Steelers in the 1970s. He enjoyed one of the greatest careers of any Penn State player and today is the only Nittany Lion to be enshrined in both the college and pro halls of fame, having earned entry to the former in 1990 and the latter in 1988. Since 2000, he has been the color analyst for the Penn State Sports Network.

The Nittany Lions developed even more great linebackers as the 1970s went on. There was **John Skorupan**, a first-team All-American who had considered attending Ohio State until meeting Woody Hayes. There was **Ed O'Neil**, a converted defensive back who helped the Nittany Lions hold their first six opponents in 1973 to a total of 32 points. There was **Lance Mehl**, lauded by Paterno as one of the program's best inside linebackers. And of course there was **Greg Buttle**, who made 343 tackles from 1973 to 1975 to become the school's career leader.

During the 1980s, the Lions added to their linebacker legacy. **Shane Conlan** was their biggest star. Like Ham, he had been lightly recruited as a prep player, having garnered little interest from big-time schools during his career at Frewsburg (N.Y.) High School. And, like Ham, he burst into the spotlight as a collegian.

The 6'3", 225-pound Conlan was famed for his relentlessness. He could blitz all day, or he could drop into pass coverage and chase down receivers. He anchored Penn State's great defenses of the mid-1980s, shining at outside linebacker in 1985 and 1986, during which the Nittany Lions went 23–1. His twisting interception of Vinny

Shane Conlan (No. 31) helped to cement the legend of Linebacker U.

Testaverde in the fourth quarter of the 1987 Fiesta Bowl turned the game in Penn State's favor. Despite playing on an injured knee, he dashed to the Miami 5-yard line to set up the Nittany Lions' winning touchdown. It was one of the biggest moments in the program's history. Conlan, a two-time first-team All-American, went on to play nine NFL seasons and attend three Pro Bowls with the Bills and Rams.

Other great players followed. Of those who took over for Conlan and company, the best was **Andre Collins**. One of 19 children from a family in Cinnaminson, New Jersey—five of whom would end up playing for Paterno—Collins gained fame in the late 1980s as a side-line-to-sideline menace. As a senior in 1989, he tied Ham's single-season record with three blocked kicks.

After a fallow four-year stretch in the late 1990s during which only one Penn State linebacker was drafted, the Nittany Lions went back to producing NFL-caliber prospects. Since 1999, two Penn Staters have won the Butkus Award, which goes to the nation's best linebacker.

In 1999, the trophy went to junior **LaVar Arrington**. In three seasons at Penn State (he left early to enter the NFL), the former prep standout from Pittsburgh became one of the most admired players in recent school history.

Arrington had been known for his spectacular feats of athleticism at North Hills High School. Penn State fans celebrated his signing and hoped he would add a dash of flair to a sometimes conservative Nittany Lion defense. He did not disappoint.

Arrington shined as a freshman and sophomore (even though he was stationed at safety his first season), and he was a holy terror as a junior. His signature moment occurred in the second half of a lopsided victory over Illinois. Guessing the snap count on fourth-and-inches, he took a running start, soared over the line of scrimmage and landed on top of running back Elmer Hickman in the backfield just as Hickman was taking the handoff. Spectators were dumbfounded, as were coaches on both sides of the field. Arrington took all the wonderment in stride. "Sometimes," he said, "you just have to take a chance."

The young linebacker took plenty of chances in his three seasons at Penn State and often drew Paterno's ire with his penchant for freelancing. Arrington took that in stride, too. He won All-America honors as a junior and was chosen second overall by the Redskins in the 2000 NFL draft, one spot behind Penn State teammate Courtney Brown.

The Nittany Lions' next Butkus Award winner had a more familiar bearing. **Paul Posluszny** was, if anything, a throwback to the days of Ham and Onkotz. Ham himself labeled Posluszny—"Puz" to his teammates—the best linebacker in school history. Nobody disputed the claim.

Like so many of Penn State's great players, Posluszny came from western Pennsylvania. He was a terrific running back and linebacker at Hopewell High just north of Pittsburgh. Though he sometimes fantasized about playing offense in college, Penn State's coaches stationed him at linebacker as a true freshman and watched as he became one of the defense's best players with his nose for the ball and tremendous closing speed. By his sophomore year, he was an established starter and a fan favorite. As a junior, he made 116 tackles and was given the Butkus Award while Penn State was preparing for its Orange Bowl appearance with Florida State, a game in which he would suffer a serious knee injury while trying to straddle a blocker.

Posluszny, who had been thinking about turning pro a year early, stuck around to rehab the injury and enjoyed a successful senior season, even though he was moved from outside linebacker to middle linebacker in a complicated depth chart chain reaction. The season was more than successful, actually. He didn't just adapt to a new position, making himself even more marketable as an NFL prospect; he broke Buttle's career tackles record along the way, snapping the 31-year-old mark in the second quarter of a game against Wisconsin in which he led the team with 14 stops.

With Posluszny, throwback that he is, now in possession of a hallowed record, Penn State's linebacker legacy has come full circle. "I played with Greg Buttle and he was one

LaVar Arrington

Paul Posluszny

heck of a football player," said defensive coordinator Tom Bradley after the game at Wisconsin. "So this couldn't happen to a more deserving, finer young man than Paul Posluszny. That's a record that will take a long time to break."

Maybe so. But the record will undoubtedly fall someday, probably to someone who plays the game a lot like Paul Posluszny. This is, after all, Linebacker U.

"So this couldn't happen to a more deserving, finer young man than Paul Posluszny."
—**TOM BRADLEY**

TAILBACKS, TOO

If there's anything Penn State fans enjoy more than watching the linebackers romp, it's watching the tailbacks romp. Although they don't have a collective nickname, the Nittany Lions' tailback graduates are as distinguished a group as the linebackers.

The first high-profile Penn State tailback was **Lenny Moore.** Nicknamed "Spats" for his high-stepping style, Moore gained 2,380 yards at Penn State in the mid-1950s. Even so, he made a bigger impression in the NFL than in the college game. He starred for the Colts in the 1950s and 1960s, making seven Pro Bowl appearances and winning enshrinement in the Pro Football Hall of Fame in 1975.

After Moore came a deluge of great Penn State runners.

Charlie Pittman was the high-revving motor that propelled the Penn State teams of 1968 and 1969 to consecutive undefeated seasons. He finished with 2,236 career yards.

Charlie Pittman

Lenny Moore

Lydell Mitchell

Following on Pittman's heels were **Lydell Mitchell** and **Franco Harris**. Talk about an embarrassment of riches. Mitchell would go on to win induction into the College Football Hall of Fame, while Harris would see his bust immortalized in Canton in 1990 after rushing for 12,120 yards for the Steelers and Seahawks. At Penn State, the two played together in the same backfield.

One could argue that the Lions' tailback tradition reached a zenith in a 1969 game with Boston College. In that 38–16 win, Harris (136 yards), Mitchell (120 yards) and Pittman (106 yards) each broke the century mark.

Improbably, the Lions' running game didn't suffer after Mitchell and Harris left. **John Cappelletti** won the Heisman Trophy in 1973 after rushing for 1,522 yards and 17 touchdowns.

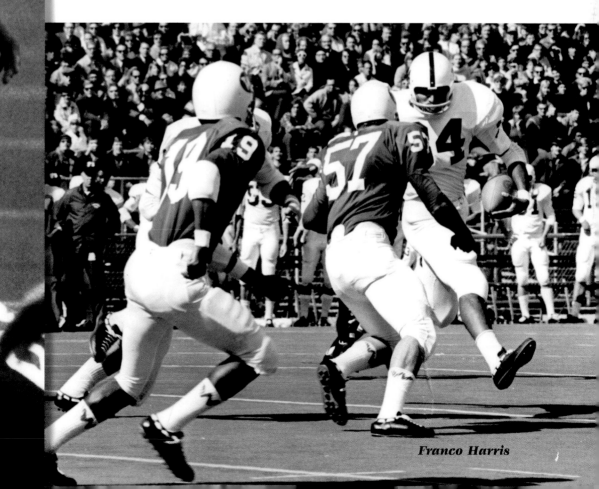

Franco Harris

In the 1980s, Penn State enjoyed another remarkable run, with **Curt Warner** passing the baton to **D.J. Dozier**, who passed it to **Blair Thomas**. All three posted top-10 finishes in Heisman Trophy voting.

It was Warner who far outshone Heisman winner Marcus Allen in Penn State's dominating 26–10 Fiesta Bowl win over USC following the 1981 season. Warner piled up 145 yards rushing—one of his Penn State-record 18 100-yard games—and scored two touchdowns.

Dozier led the Lions in rushing in all four of his seasons in Happy Valley, including the 1986 national championship season. Dozier scored the decisive touchdown in Penn State's 14–10 win over Miami.

Thomas was at his best in a 21–20 upset of seventh-ranked Notre Dame in 1987, rushing for 214 yards on 35 tough carries.

In the 1990s, **Ki-Jana Carter** emerged as one of the brightest stars in an offense that some regard as the best in college football history. Recruited in 1991 along with two other able runners, Mike

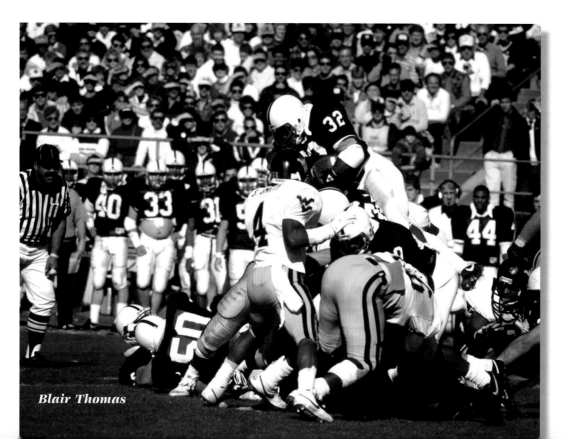

Blair Thomas

Ki-Jana Carter

Archie and Stephen Pitts, Carter separated himself from the pack with his miraculous speed and deceptive strength. He set the tone for the 1995 Rose Bowl when, on the first play from scrimmage, he crashed through a hole on the right side of the line and sprinted past the entire Oregon defense for an 83-yard touchdown.

Following Carter's departure, the Lions continued to find effective running backs. **Curtis Enis** was a punishing runner from Ohio who preferred to bowl over tacklers rather than avoid them. He led the Lions in rushing from 1995 to 1997. Enis would be remembered more fondly by Penn State fans had he not taken a suit and other gifts from an agent, forcing school officials to declare him ineligible for the team's 1998 Citrus Bowl appearance against Florida.

The Lions' next great runner didn't emerge until 2002. His name was **Larry Johnson**, and he was one angry young tailback. Johnson attacked every play as if he had something to prove. He was the son of Penn State's defensive line coach and felt he needed to silence the whispers that he was on scholarship only because of his father. After sitting behind a dependable runner named Eric McCoo for most of his career, he did just what he set out to do. Johnson finished his senior season with 2,087 yards, becoming the first player in the 107-year history of the Big Ten to surpass 2,000 yards rushing in the regular season. Onlookers were taken aback,

Curtis Enis

PENN STATE'S TAILBACK LEGACY
THE 2,000-YARD RUSHERS

NAME	YDS.	TDS	HEISMAN FINISH
Curt Warner, 1979–1982	3,398	24	10th, 1982
Tony Hunt, 2003–2006	3,320	25	
Blair Thomas, 1985–1987, 1989	3,301	21	10th, 1989
Curtis Enis, 1995–1997	3,256	36	6th, 1997
D.J. Dozier, 1983–1986	3,227	25	8th, 1986
Larry Johnson, 1999–2002	2,953	26	3rd, 2002
Lydell Mitchell, 1969–1971	2,934	38	5th, 1971
Ki-Jana Carter, 1992–1994	2,829	34	2nd, 1994
Matt Suhey, 1976–1979	2,818	26	
John Cappelletti, 1972–1973	2,639	29	
Eric McCoo, 1998–2001	2,518	18	
Lenny Moore, 1953–1955	2,380	23	
Charlie Pittman, 1967–1969	2,236	30	
Booker Moore, 1977–1980	2,072	20	
Jon Williams, 1980–1983	2,042	14	
Franco Harris, 1969–1971	2,002	24	

Paterno among them. "Larry Johnson is one of the greatest football players I've been around," he gushed, "if not the greatest."

If there's been a knock on Penn State's tailbacks during the past 20 years it's that, with the exception of Johnson, the high-profile backs haven't succeeded in the NFL. Whether due to injuries (Carter, Thomas), disinterest (Dozier) or some combination of the two (Enis), an inexplicably high number of Penn State tailback prospects have gone bust in the NFL. "There are guys who were great [college] players who've had no success [in the NFL], and there are guys who I didn't think would be able to make a team who are in their fourth or fifth years," said former Penn State offensive coordinator Fran Ganter. "I am amazed sometimes, so I've given up guessing."

Still, there's no denying their success at the college level. Penn State might not have enough star power to wrest the "Tailback U." title from Southern California, but its best runners can hold their own with just about anyone.

JOHN CAPPELLETTI

Running Back
1971–1973
Inducted 1993

See The Heisman Trophy Winner, page 3.

KEITH DORNEY

Offensive Tackle
1975–1978
Inducted 2005

It took a while for Dorney to find a permanent spot on the Penn State depth chart. But once he did, he thrived. The Macungie, Pennsylvania, native played tight end as a true freshman and made his first career start in the 1975 Sugar Bowl against Alabama. By the start of the 1976 season, he was a center. A year later, he was a tackle. Other players might have struggled to adapt to the frequent changes, but Dorney excelled. Penn State went 22–2 during his two years as a starter. During that time, Dorney became one of only 12 Nittany Lions to twice earn first-team All-America recognition.

KEITH DORNEY AT A GLANCE

- 6'5", 256 pounds
- Unanimous All-America selection in 1978, when he helped lead the Lions to an unbeaten regular season
- Selected by the Detroit Lions with the tenth-overall selection in the 1979 NFL Draft
- Played nine NFL seasons, all with the Lions

"Jack Ham's career is a monument to the work ethic. He was not a highly recruited athlete, but his exceptional intelligence and capacity for hard work made him an extraordinary football player. I don't think any of us knew then what an enormous talent we were getting. Jack Ham will always be the consummate Penn Stater."
—JOE PATERNO

JACK HAM

Linebacker
1968–1970
Inducted 1990

See Linebacker U., page 7.

JACK HAM AT A GLANCE

- 6'3", 212 pounds
- 251 career tackles (143 solo)
- Second-round draft pick of the Steelers in 1971
- Four-time Super Bowl winner with Pittsburgh
- 1975 NFL Defensive Player of the Year

GLENN KILLINGER
Quarterback
1918, 1920–1921
Inducted 1971

Killinger wasn't allowed to play football in high school because he was considered too small. By the time he got to Penn State, he stood 5'9", 167 pounds. With so few men on campus due to World War I, coach Hugo Bezdek held open tryouts and Killinger made the team. He became a nine-time letterman in football, basketball and baseball, led Penn State to consecutive unbeaten seasons and was named to the Walter Camp All-America team in 1921.

GLENN KILLINGER AT A GLANCE

- 5'9", 167 pounds
- Led Penn State to unbeaten records in 1920 and 1921
- Walter Camp All-American as a senior
- Killinger captained Penn State football and basketball teams; he was on the baseball team and won 30 consecutive games as a pitcher.
- Overall record as a college head coach: 170–70–15

Glenn Killinger

TED KWALICK
Tight End
1966–1968
Inducted 1989

A sure-handed pass-catcher and tenacious
blocker, Kwalick was one of the biggest
stars of the early Paterno era. Indeed,
there might not have been much of a
Paterno era had he not caught nine
passes for 89 yards in Penn State's 17–8
victory over Miami in September 1967. At
the time, Penn State's second-year coach
was worried about his job security and
felt he needed to scrap his depth chart
and turn to a group of unknown sopho-
mores, a group that included Kwalick. It
proved to be a wise decision. Kwalick
became a two-time first-team All-
American, the first Penn State player to
be so honored since Bob Higgins in 1919.
In the 1969 Orange Bowl, his final college
game, he caught six passes for 74 yards.

TED KWALICK
AT A GLANCE

- 6'4", 225 pounds
- Career totals of 1,343 yards
  receiving and 10 touchdowns
- Career-long reception was an
  89-yarder against Miami in 1968
- Nine-year pro career with San
  Francisco and Oakland
- Of Kwalick, Joe Paterno once said,
  "He's what God had in mind when
  he made a football player."

Ted Kwalick

Rich Lucas

RICH LUCAS
1957–1959
Quarterback
Inducted 1986

The dashing Lucas was one of Rip Engle's biggest stars. As a senior, he guided the Lions to a 9–2 record, leading them in rushing (325 yards) and passing (913 yards). He called his own plays and often called his own number. Lucas is regarded as one of the best running quarterbacks in school history, a deft scrambler who could also get the tough yards when he had to. In contrast to its future policy under Paterno, Penn State aggressively promoted Lucas for postseason awards. Newspapers had taken to calling him "Riverboat Richie," and the school's sports information office embraced the publicity. Penn State officials went so far as to pose Lucas in 19th-century riverboat gambling garb, complete with a bow tie, bowler, arm garter and a deck of cards. The aim was to garner some national attention. Whether due to the publicists' tireless efforts, Lucas' marvelous play or some combination of the two, it worked. He won the Maxwell Award, was a first-team All-American and finished second in balloting for the Heisman Trophy in 1959, to LSU's Billy Cannon.

EUGENE "SHORTY" MILLER

Quarterback
1910-1913
Inducted 1974

Not for nothing was Miller called "Shorty." Standing 5'5", 140 pounds, he was diminutive even by the standards of the day. But he was tough and quick. In Penn State's 1911 season opener, he dashed 95 yards with the opening kickoff. Newspapers began referring to him as the "Meteoric Midget." Miller went on to start four seasons, leading Penn State to an 8–0 record in 1912. He ended up playing three years of professional football with the Massillon (Ohio) Tigers.

SHORTY MILLER AT A GLANCE

- 5'5", 145 pounds
- Sparkplug of two undefeated seasons
- Missed only one game during his four-year career at Penn State as the Lions went 23–8–2
- Known for imitating his coach, Jack Hollenback, by giving intense pep talks in his coach's voice and keeping his teammates loose

Eugene "Shorty" Miller

LYDELL MITCHELL

Running Back
1969–1971
Inducted 2004

See Tailbacks, Too, page 19.

LYDELL MITCHELL
AT A GLANCE

- 5'11", 204 pounds
- In 1971, he set NCAA records with 29 total touchdowns and 174 points, while shattering the school record with 1,567 rushing yards, earning first-team All-America honors and finishing fifth in voting for the Heisman Trophy.
- Outstanding Player of the 1972 Cotton Bowl, a 30–6 win over Texas
- Amassed 2,934 career rushing yards and 38 touchdowns—both school records at the time
- Successful 10-year pro career with three teams

DENNIS ONKOTZ

Linebacker
1967–1969
Inducted 1995

See Linebacker U., page 7.

DENNIS ONKOTZ
AT A GLANCE

- 6'2", 212 pounds
- All-American in 1968 and 1969, when Penn State enjoyed two straight 11–0 seasons, including bowl wins over Kansas and Missouri
- During his three seasons as LB, he intercepted 11 passes and ran three interceptions for touchdowns
- Also returned 47 punts for an average of 13.2 yards
- Led the team in tackles with 71 in 1968, and 97 in 1969
- Academic All-American in 1969

PETE MAUTHE

Fullback
1909–1912
Inducted 1957

Mauthe was an all-purpose player for Penn State when the program was just starting to get off the ground. He was a great running back and scored 119 points as a senior, leading the team to an 8–0 record. Mauthe was also a fine kicker and punter. During his senior season, he kicked a 51-yard field goal.

PETE MAUTHE
AT A GLANCE

- Led Penn State to a 26–2–4 record during his time in Happy Valley
- Beat Pitt 3–0 with a 35-yard field goal in 1911
- Scored 119 of the team's 285 points during the unbeaten 1912 season
- Established a scholarship at Penn State for engineering students

MIKE REID

Defensive Tackle
1967–1969
Inducted 1987

Reid is one of the most fascinating figures in Penn State history. It's hard to believe that one person could be so proficient at so many things. A ferocious defender, he won the Outland Trophy as a senior and remains the only Penn Stater to be named the country's outstanding interior lineman. He also wrestled for Penn State, winning the Eastern heavyweight title in 1967. After college, he played five NFL seasons, all with the Bengals, and went to two Pro Bowls. Slowed by knee injuries, he decided to give up football after the 1974 season and turned his attention to his other great love: music. With help from his friend Larry Gatlin, another football player turned country music star, Reid became a prolific songwriter. He wrote 11 No. 1 hits in the 1980s and won the Grammy Award for best country song in 1984. He is the only Nittany Lion player to be enshrined in both the College Football Hall of Fame and the Nashville Songwriters Hall of Fame.

MIKE REID
AT A GLANCE

- 6'3", 240 pounds
- In 1969, as a senior, Reid made 89 tackles, was a unanimous All-America choice, won the Outland Trophy as the outstanding interior lineman in America, and was awarded the Maxwell Trophy as the nation's outstanding player in college football.
- Twice named All-Pro with the Cincinnati Bengals
- Grammy Award-winning songwriter

Mike Reid

Glenn Ressler

GLENN RESSLER
Guard
1962–1964
Inducted 2001

A two-way lineman, Ressler was a terror no matter where he lined up. He played center and middle guard, anchoring both lines during the latter days of Engle's reign as head coach. He was a consensus All-American his senior year and was named the nation's top player by the Maxwell Football Club. Ressler later enjoyed a 10-year NFL career with the Colts, for whom he played in two Super Bowls.

GLENN RESSLER AT A GLANCE

- 6'3", 250 pounds
- In 1964, he became only the fifth lineman to win the Maxwell Award given to the nation's best player.
- Named All-East twice and consensus All-American in 1964
- Had 15 unassisted tackles as the Nittany Lions upset top-ranked Ohio State 26–0 in 1963
- 10-year pro career with the Baltimore Colts

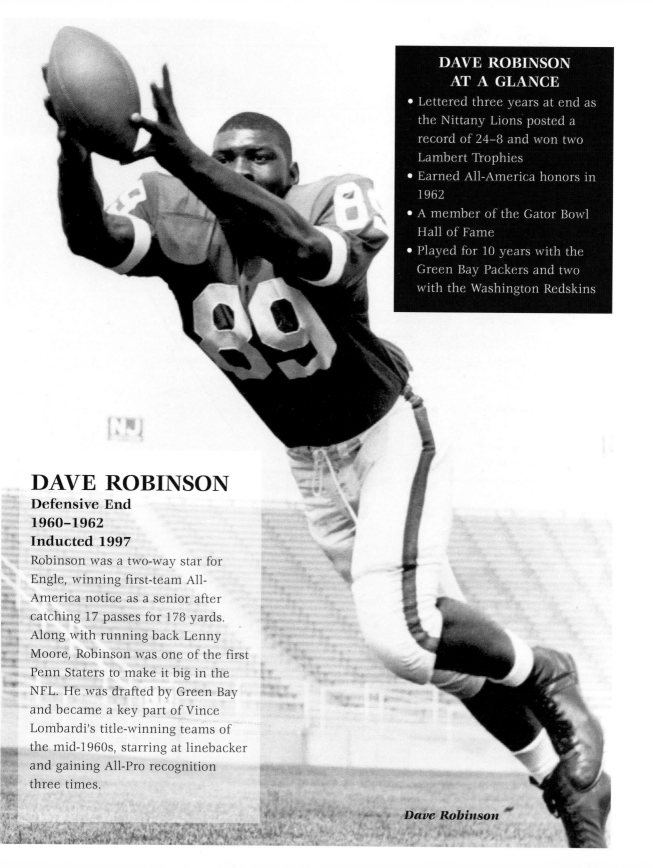

DAVE ROBINSON

Defensive End
1960–1962
Inducted 1997

Robinson was a two-way star for Engle, winning first-team All-America notice as a senior after catching 17 passes for 178 yards. Along with running back Lenny Moore, Robinson was one of the first Penn Staters to make it big in the NFL. He was drafted by Green Bay and became a key part of Vince Lombardi's title-winning teams of the mid-1960s, starring at linebacker and gaining All-Pro recognition three times.

Dave Robinson

STEVE SUHEY

Guard

1942, 1946–1947

Inducted 1985

The Suhey family has deep connections to Penn State. It all began when Steve returned from the Pacific after a three-year tour of duty with the Army Air Corps during World War II. Re-enrolling at Penn State, he became one of the stars of Bob Higgins' unbeaten 1947 team, which finished fourth in the country. Suhey went on to play two NFL seasons with the Steelers. He married Higgins' daughter, Virginia, and the couple had seven children, three of whom—Larry, Paul and Matt—played for Paterno in the 1970s, with Matt going on to enjoy a long NFL career with the Bears.

Steve Suhey

STEVE SUHEY AT A GLANCE

- 5'11", 205 pounds
- Earned All-America honors in 1947
- Career interrupted by three years of service in the Air Corps during World War II
- Three of his sons—Larry, Paul, and Matt—earned letters at Penn State from 1975–1979

DEXTER VERY
End
1909–1912
Inducted 1976

Very was one of Penn State's earliest stars and one of its most durable. He is remembered for having never missed a game in his career. Some say he was never removed from a game for any reason even though he played offense and defense, and he refused to wear a helmet. Very caught passes and returned kickoffs and punts. His 70-yard punt return against Penn in 1911 established a school record that stood for 22 years. He also competed for the wrestling team, losing only two bouts in four years.

DEXTER VERY AT A GLANCE

- Started every game of his four-year career
- Lions lost only two games during those four years, posting three unbeaten seasons
- Led Penn State to its first win over Penn in 18 years by snatching the ball from the grasp of a Penn player and scoring a touchdown
- Scored nine touchdowns in eight games in 1912
- Never wore headgear

HARRY "LIGHT HORSE" WILSON
Halfback
1921–1923
Inducted 1973

Wilson was a remarkable man. He scored every touchdown for Penn State in the final six games of the 1923 season and was named an All-American. Leaving Penn State for Army the following year, he became an All-American for his new team, leading it in scoring in consecutive seasons. After receiving his commission in 1928, he became an airman and flew 45 combat missions as a pilot commander in the Army Air Corps in World War II, winning the Distinguished Flying Cross and the Air Medal with five oak leaf clusters. He retired from the service in 1956 and lived another 34 years.

HARRY WILSON AT A GLANCE

- 5'9", 170 pounds
- Walter Camp: "Wilson on his good days has no peer."
- In 1923, he had touchdown runs against Navy of 95, 80 and 55 yards and against Pennsylvania of 49, 45 and 25 yards.
- Flew 45 missions as a bomber pilot in World War II

Dexter Very

Harry "Light Horse" Wilson

TODD BLACKLEDGE
Quarterback
1980–1982

A native of Canton, Ohio, Blackledge had football in his blood. He became a starter in the fourth game of his sophomore year and held the position for the rest of his career. Although he had a penchant for interceptions (he threw 41 in his career, more than any QB in school history), he also was one of the school's most productive quarterbacks, winning the Davey O'Brien Award his senior year when he led the Lions to their first national championship. After leaving school a year early, Blackledge was taken by Kansas City in the quarterback-rich draft of 1983. He never scaled the heights of fellow first-rounders Dan Marino, John Elway and Jim Kelly, but he reinvented himself as a broadcaster and is now one of the nation's most respected college football analysts.

SEASON	YARDS	ATT.	CMP.	INT.	TD
1980	1,037	159	76	13	7
1981	1,557	207	104	14	12
1982	2,218	292	161	14	22
Career	4,812	658	341	41	41

KERRY COLLINS
Quarterback
1991–1994

Dogged by injuries and inconsistency, Collins battled John Sacca at the start of his career. But when his disgruntled rival abruptly left the team midway through the 1993 season, he began to flourish. As a senior, Collins enjoyed the greatest season of any quarterback in school history. He orchestrated the Lions' brilliant offensive showing of 1994, completing 67 percent of his passes for a school-record 2,679 yards. Following his graduation, NFL scouts complained of a "hitch" in Collins' delivery, but it didn't prevent Carolina from choosing him with the fifth overall pick in the 1995 draft, nor did it stop Collins from playing 12 NFL seasons to date, one of which (2000) ended in a Super Bowl appearance with the Giants.

SEASON	YARDS	ATT.	CMP.	INT.	TD
1991	95	6	3	1	1
1992	925	137	64	2	4
1993	1,605	250	127	11	13
1994	2,679	264	176	7	21
Career	5,304	657	370	21	39

Kerry Collins

CHUCK FUSINA
Quarterback
1976–1978

Another great western Pennsylvania player, Fusina came out of McKees Rocks to lead the Nittany Lions to the brink of a national championship. He had his most decorated season as a senior, throwing for 1,859 yards and 11 touchdowns and winning the Maxwell Award as the nation's outstanding player. Although he played five NFL seasons, Fusina made a bigger impression in the fledgling USFL, where he teamed with fellow Penn Stater Scott Fitzkee to lead the Philadelphia/Baltimore Stars to two league championships.

SEASON	YARDS	ATT.	CMP.	INT.	TD
1975	42	9	4	1	0
1976	1,260	168	88	10	11
1977	2,221	246	142	9	15
1978	1,859	242	137	12	11
Career	5,382	665	371	32	37

During Chuck Fusina's junior and senior seasons, the Lions went 22–2, with the two losses coming by a total of 11 points.

BOBBY ENGRAM
Wide Receiver
1991, 1993–1995

Engram got off to a terrible start at Penn State. He was a teammate's unwitting accomplice in a petty burglary and sat out a year as punishment. But Paterno thought the incident seemed out of character and gave the young receiver a second chance, hoping he would redeem himself. Boy, did he redeem himself. Engram went on to become the greatest wideout in Penn State history, catching 167 passes for 3,026 yards, both school records. He has played 11 NFL seasons, six with the Seahawks, and is active in a number of charities.

SEASON	REC.	YARDS	AVG.	TD
1991	4	40	10.0	0
1993	48	873	18.2	13
1994	52	1,029	19.8	7
1995	63	1,084	17.2	11
Career	167	3,026	18.1	31

Wide receiver Bobby Engram was a catalyst for some of the most explosive offensive units in Penn State history. In four bowl games, all of them Nittany Lion routs, Engram caught 16 passes for 272 yards (17.0-yard average) and three touchdowns.

MATT MILLEN
Defensive Tackle
1976–1979

Millen was a brash young lineman who didn't always agree with Paterno and wasn't afraid to say so. Their spats were legendary, and Paterno once threw him off the team for refusing to complete a conditioning run. But the coach couldn't afford to be without him. Indeed, when Millen and partner Bruce Clark were injured as seniors, the defense suffered and Penn State fell to 8–4. After graduating, Millen became a stalwart NFL lineman with the Raiders, 49ers and Redskins. He won a Super Bowl with each of those teams (four in all) before losing his Midas touch as CEO of the Lions.

BRUCE CLARK
Defensive Tackle
1976–1979

Paired with Matt Millen on the Lions' great defensive lines of the late 1970s, Clark was the less controversial half of the feared "Salt and Pepper" tackle tandem. His junior and senior years, he blew up plays with ruthless abandon. Clark won the Lombardi Award in 1978 and might as well have been up for the Doak Walker Award, too, considering how much time he spent in opponents' backfields. Of his 51 tackles that season, 21 resulted in losses and four were sacks. Clark suffered a knee injury late in his senior year, but he did have a lengthy pro career in the NFL, CFL and World League of American Football.

NEAL SMITH
Safety
1967–1969

Smith came to Penn State as a walk-on and left as an All-American. An unknown from tiny Port Trevorton, Pa., he was the most unlikely star on Penn State's great defenses of the late 1960s. Although he played at a time when freshmen were ineligible, he is still the school's career leader with 19 interceptions.

Neal Smith

The team is a reflection of the man. There's nobody like JoePa, and there's no team like the Nittany Lions.

The Great Coaches

Since 1950, Penn State has made exactly one coaching change. Think about that for a moment. Penn State is so well known for the durability of its current coaching staff that it's easy to forget the Lions have had more than one iconic coach. Fourteen men have coached the team since its inception in 1887, and a number of them enjoyed great success. Four of Penn State's past five coaches are in the National Football Foundation College Hall of Fame. Here's a look at some of the most important names in the program's history.

"I consider myself, and I know my teammates and Penn State players past and present feel likewise, a better person for having played for Joe Paterno."

**—FORMER QUARTERBACK AND
CURRENT TELEVISION
ANALYST TODD BLACKLEDGE**

GEORGE HOSKINS
1892–1895
Record at Penn State: 17–4–4

The first five seasons of Penn State football were informal, to say the least. The team didn't have a full-time coach and rarely ventured far beyond its isolated central Pennsylvania redoubt. Its first season consisted of a home-and-home series against Bucknell. Its most arduous road trips the next three years were to Penn and Dickinson.

It wasn't until the early 1890s that school officials, long focused on upgrading the academic credentials of their small, agricultural institution, turned their attention to athletics. One of their first moves was to hire Hoskins.

A Vermont native, Hoskins was brought in to teach physical education. As part of the job, he was required to coach the football team, and coach it he did. After a 20–0 loss at Penn to open the 1892 season, the Lions easily won their remaining five games, outscoring their opponents by a cumulative score of 108–0.

Over the next two seasons, the team would go 10–1–1 and Hoskins would see his stature rise within the burgeoning profession of college coaching. It rose so high that Penn State couldn't keep him around any longer. He took a job coaching at the school that would become Pitt and later served as a trainer for the Cincinnati Reds. Hoskins died in 1957, but not before helping lay the groundwork for a football dynasty.

GEORGE HOSKINS AT A GLANCE	
YEAR	RECORD
1892	5–1
1893	4–1
1894	6–0–1
1895	2–2–3

HUGO BEZDEK
1918–1929
65–30–11

Bezdek was a renaissance man, a Zelig-like figure who frequently found himself in close proximity to the people and events that shaped the American spectator-sports culture of the early 20th century. A native of Czechoslovakia, he learned the game from the legendary Amos Alonzo Stagg at the University of Chicago. Bezdek eventually followed Stagg into coaching and led Oregon to the Rose Bowl. Later, he took over the Pittsburgh Pirates baseball club, turning it into a pennant contender.

It was while Bezdek was in Pittsburgh that Penn State officials approached him about becoming the school's football coach. Penn State had lost five in a row to Pitt, and officials were eager to find a strategist who could match wits with the Panthers' genius-in-residence, Pop Warner. Bezdek was that strategist. He had developed the screen pass and other innovations earlier in his coaching career. As historian Lou Prato explains in his *Penn State Football Encyclopedia,* Bezdek was viewed as potential savior when he agreed to take the job. And through the first few years of his stay in University Park, no one had cause to complain.

Under Bezdek, the Lions ended Pitt's winning streak. They shut out the heralded Panthers, 20–0, at Forbes Field in 1919. As an anonymous wordsmith put it, writing for *The Pittsburgh Press,* "the Mountain Lions feasted sumptuously upon Panther meat—and picked their teeth with the shinbones of a Warner eleven."

The Lions would go on to enjoy nine winning seasons under Bezdek. After the 1922 regular season, he led them to their first bowl game, a Rose Bowl appearance in which they lost, 14–3, to Southern California.

But the Warner eleven would have its revenge. Following the 1919 upset, Bezdek never again defeated Pitt. His record against the Panthers was 1–9–2. That, coupled with a brusque manner that alienated associates, led to his departure as coach.

HUGO BEZDEK AT A GLANCE	
YEAR	RECORD
1918	1–2–1
1919	7–1
1920	7–0–2
1921	8–0–2
1922	6–4–1
1923	6–2–1
1924	6–3–1
1925	4–4–1
1926	5–4
1927	6–2–1
1928	3–5–1
1929	6–3

BOB HIGGINS
1930–1948
91–57–11

A star player under Bezdek, Higgins rescued the Nittany Lions from the darkest period in their history. Toward the end of the 1920s, the university began de-emphasizing athletics. As part of its plan, scholarships were discontinued. The decision had disastrous consequences for the burgeoning football program, which until then was shaping up as one of the best in the East.

Forced to survive without financial aid, Higgins' first two teams went a combined 5–12–2. Alumni began grumbling that the Lions needed a new coach. Higgins disagreed. He thought they needed new players.

He was right. And eventually, he figured out how to get those players. As Prato explains in his *Penn State Football Encyclopedia,* Higgins began working with alumni to overcome the school's restrictions on sports scholarships. When Penn State found a player it wanted, the alums would swoop in to offer him a job to help pay for school. Bookstores would loan textbooks to players, and fraternities would hold raffles to fund the training table. It was ethically dubious, but in those lean times, Penn State's coaches did what they had to do.

The Lions bottomed out in the 1930s, going 29–40–4 in Higgins' first nine seasons. But once he began stockpiling high school talent, he showed what kind of coach he was. He built the team into a winner in his second decade and went on to coach it to one of its greatest seasons ever. In 1947, the Lions went 9–0–1, tied SMU in the Cotton Bowl and finished fourth in the nation.

Higgins retired after the 1948 season citing health concerns. He had suffered from heart problems and watched as longtime assistant Joe Bedenk was promoted to head coach. In 1954, he was enshrined in the College Football Hall of Fame.

The Lions had their ups downs under Higgins, never more so than in 1938. "All season we have been alternating, paying well one Saturday and poorly the next," he said following a 7–7 tie against favored Penn. "This was our Saturday to play well, and I think we did." He couldn't have known it at the time, but the program he was building would become a model of consistency. The Lions went 3–4–1 in 1938. It would be 50 years before they were to suffer another losing season.

BOB HIGGINS AT A GLANCE	
YEAR	RECORD
1930	3–4–2
1931	2–8
1932	2–5
1933	3–3–1
1934	4–4
1935	4–4
1936	3–5
1937	5–3
1938	3–4–1
1939	5–1–2
1940	6–1–1
1941	7–2
1942	6–1–1
1943	5–3–1
1944	6–3
1945	5–3
1946	6–2
1947	9–0–1
1948	7–1–1

RIP ENGLE
1950–1965
104–48–4

Engle is probably best remembered for hiring a bespectacled Brooklyn kid as an assistant coach in 1950. But he did much more than simply set the stage for Penn State's glory years by inviting Joe Paterno to join him in University Park; he enjoyed a bit of glory himself.

Engle had grown up in Pennsylvania. He was born in 1906 in Elk Lick, a tiny coal town in the hills of Somerset County, and took his first job in the mines at age 14 driving mules. Engle later became a star defensive end at Western Maryland and turned to coaching after graduation, guiding Waynesboro (Pennsylvania) High to eight conference championships in 11 seasons.

His success in Waynesboro led to a stint at Brown, where Engle proved just as adept at coaching collegians. He developed an especially good rapport with the Paterno brothers. Joe was the quarterback, younger brother George the fullback. George was a strapping athlete, the recipient of a scholarship offer from Boston College. But Engle saw something he liked in the skinny older brother, of whom it was once said, "He can't run, can't pass. He just thinks and wins."

Engle asked Joe Paterno to join him at Penn State. The two enlisted Bedenk and his entire assistant coaching staff—university officials insisted that everyone be retained—and began building on the foundation Higgins had laid. The new coach went 5–3–1 in his first season, finishing with a 21–20 victory over host Pitt, always a good way to end a season. After that, the Lions just kept getting better, acquiring more talent, forging relationships with high school coaches in the steel mill towns to the west and coal towns to the east. Penn State was awarding scholarships again, and the administration was eager for athletic glory. Engle happily obliged. He recruited running back Lenny Moore, a future Pro Football Hall of Famer, and Richie Lucas, who would finish second in the Heisman Trophy balloting as a senior.

Slowly, steadily, the Lions were becoming a power under Engle. The team went to four consecutive bowl games from 1959–1962, defeating Alabama, Oregon and Georgia Tech before seeing its postseason winning streak end with a 17–7 loss to Florida in the Gator Bowl in 1962.

Toward the end of his tenure as head coach, Engle let Paterno exert more authority. It was clear that the team's ambitious quarterbacks coach was being groomed for the position. Engle, concerned about his health and eager to begin his retirement, decided he would step down after the 1965 season. His last team went

RIP ENGLE AT A GLANCE	
YEAR	RECORD
1950	5–3–1
1951	5–4
1952	7–2–1
1953	6–3
1954	7–2
1955	5–4
1956	6–2–1
1957	6–3
1958	6–3–1
1959	9–2
1960	7–3
1961	8–3
1962	9–2
1963	7–3
1964	6–4
1965	5–5

a disappointing 5–5. Soon after Penn State closed out its season with a 19–7 victory at Maryland, he announced his decision. It was the end of an era.

Engle died on March 7, 1983, nine years after his election to the College Football Hall of Fame and two months after Penn State won its first national championship. In his 16 seasons at University Park, he proved himself above all a sportsman. "A team that defeats a far inferior team has accomplished nothing," he once said. The Lions took those words to heart. Under Engle, they sought out challenges in hopes of overcoming the national media's disdain for Eastern football. Following a heartbreaking 20–18 loss to fourth-ranked Syracuse in 1959, Engle visited the Orange locker room to congratulate their players. They responded with a hearty round of applause. Penn State fans understood perfectly the sentiment.

"I don't think our uniforms look that bad. I think they say something to kids about team-oriented play and an austere approach to life."
—PATERNO ON PENN STATE'S CONSERVATIVE LOOK—DARK JERSEYS WITHOUT PLAYER NAMES, PLAIN WHITE HELMETS, BLACK SHOES

JOE PATERNO

1966–present
363–121–3

Where to begin? Paterno is synonymous with Penn State football in
much the same way that Bear
Bryant is linked forever to Alabama,
John Wooden to UCLA and Vince
Lombardi to the Green Bay Packers.
He ranks second in all-time Division
I-A coaching victories and is within
reach of the leader, Florida State's
Bobby Bowden. He has enjoyed five
unbeaten seasons and won two
national championships. He's
coached 71 first-team All-Americans,
seven College Hall of Famers and 30
first-round NFL draft picks. Three of
his former players—Jack Ham, Mike
Munchak and Franco Harris—are
enshrined in Canton. He's a Hall of
Famer himself, having been
inducted into the college hall in
December 2006. People like to think
the Nittany Lions don't have an
emblem, but the truth is they do.
It's Paterno. Just try to imagine this
program without visions of JoePa's
wavy pompadour or rolled-up
trouser legs creeping into your sub-
conscious. Go ahead, try. Not so
easy, is it?

The on-field highlights of
Paterno's career are so familiar they
hardly bear repeating. There's the
breakthrough 1968 season, in which
the Lions went 11–0 and emerged as

something more than just another regional power; the marvelous 1969 encore in which they matched their previous record by going unbeaten and defeating Missouri, 10–3, in the Orange Bowl; the national championship seasons of 1982 and 1986; the unbeaten 1994 season in which the Lions fielded what some regard as the best offense in college football history yet finished second to Nebraska in both polls; and, of course, the magical 29–27 victory over Ohio State in 2001, which gave Paterno his 324th career win, one more than Bryant amassed in his career.

What makes Paterno's career so interesting is that none of those triumphs ever seemed preordained. The very idea that this lawyer's son would become a football coach was absurd. And not just to friends and family, but to Paterno himself. He was planning on attending law school.

A surprise phone call from Engle changed Paterno's life. But even after taking up coaching at Penn State—the only postgraduate employer he has ever known—his ascent to the top of the profession was fraught with road blocks and detours. In 1967, his second season, Penn State lost its opener to Navy, 23–22, on a freak play. Coming on the heels of a 5–5 debut season, the loss shook the faith of some early Paterno backers. All of a sudden, Rip's boy wonder didn't seem so smart. "I thought I was going to get fired," Paterno recalled recently. "A kid by the name of John Sladki from Johnstown...they threw a pass on the last play of the game, he deflected it and the guy caught it and ran. I go to bed sometimes thinking about Sladki, poor guy." School officials stuck by their young coach. He justified their faith by guiding Penn State to victories in 31 of its next 33 games.

But there were more difficulties to come. An Alabama goal-line stand in the Sugar Bowl cost top-ranked Penn State the 1978 national championship and gave rise to talk that Paterno couldn't win the big one. It remains the most haunting loss of the Paterno era. And while Paterno did finally get even with the Bear—more than even, actually—his triumph had a bittersweet aftertaste. Even as he was eclipsing Bryant's career victories record in October 2001, the Lions were in the midst of their second consecutive losing season. From 2000 to 2004, Penn State would suffer four losing seasons. It was the school's longest period of sustained mediocrity since the 1930s.

"One of the greatest things Coach Paterno has said, when asked about his greatest team, is 'I don't know. I'll tell you in 20 years.' He really believes his greatest team isn't which one had the fewest losses. His greatest team is what becomes of the men he coached. That's a rarity in collegiate and professional sports, but that just epitomizes the class and values of Coach Paterno."

—STEVE WISNIEWSKI, GUARD, 1985–1988

Still, Paterno avoided some other trap doors. He resisted the urge to leave for the NFL, spurning an offer from the Patriots in the early 1970s. He didn't venture into politics as some other legendary sports figures have done, nor did he fall victim to health problems typically associated with high-pressure jobs. Even after suffering a broken leg in November 2006 when a player ran into him on the sideline at Wisconsin, he tried to talk his doctor into letting him coach the team's next game a week later against Temple. The doctor refused, but the incident said volumes about Paterno's determination. Said defensive coordinator Tom Bradley, "He's a wily old rascal. He's not going anywhere."

Paterno's only real indulgence—if that's what it is—is his desire to keep on working. With the losing seasons a not-so-distant memory, some would like to see him step away. Forty-one years, they say, should be enough for anyone.

But that wily old rascal has built up an enormous reservoir of goodwill in his tenure as head coach. He may not be the saintly figure the national media makes him out to be. He may be cranky and stubborn, and he may scapegoat the officials from time to time in a way that some find unseemly. But he graduates his players, he gives back to the university (more than $4 million in philanthropic contributions as of this writing) and he lends the football program an iconic dimension it might otherwise lack.

Oh, and he still wins games in bunches from time to time. In 2005, the Nittany Lions went 11–1 and defeated Florida State, 26–23, in a triple-overtime Orange Bowl marathon. After the game, senior quarterback Michael Robinson took a seat in the interview room and addressed Paterno's critics. He was speaking specifically about the recent attacks on the coach's fitness for command, but he could just as well have been addressing an earlier generation of skeptics, those who thought Paterno was too stodgy or archaic or conservative to succeed.

"To think that people actually wanted him to give this game up, to call it quits, when we knew what type of team we could have, I mean, I'm at a loss for words," Robinson said. "What could these people have been thinking?"

"I think everyone on the team not only wanted to win the Big Ten but to show the nation that the program was back and that Coach Paterno still had it, that he's able to do things the right way with the right guys and not bend or break any rules. To get back in the spotlight, I think all of the players just wanted that for Coach."

—LINEBACKER PAUL POSLUSZNY,
ON THE 2005 SEASON

YEAR	RECORD	FINAL AP RANKING
1966	5–5	
1967	8–2–1	10th
1968	11–0	2nd
1969	11–0	2nd
1970	7–3	18th
1971	11–1	5th
1972	10–2	10th
1973	12–0	5th
1974	10–2	7th
1975	9–3	10th
1976	7–5	
1977	11–1	5th
1978	11–1	4th
1979	8–4	20th
1980	10–2	8th
1981	10–2	3rd
1982	11–1	1st
1983	8–4–1	
1984	6–5	
1985	11–1	3rd
1986	12–0	1st
1987	8–4	
1988	5–6	
1989	8–3–1	15th
1990	9–3	11th
1991	11–2	3rd
1992	7–5	
1993	10–2	8th
1994	12–0	2nd
1995	9–3	13th
1996	11–2	7th
1997	9–3	16th
1998	9–3	17th
1999	10–3	11th
2000	5–7	
2001	5–6	
2002	9–4	16th
2003	3–9	
2004	4–7	
2005	11–1	3rd
2006	9–4	24th

JOE PATERNO AT A GLANCE

PATERNO TIMELINE

1949 *With his brother George, Paterno leads Brown to an 8-1 record as a senior.*

1950 *Paterno joins Rip Engle's staff at Penn State as an assistant coach.*

1966 *On Feb. 19, Paterno is named Engle's successor and 14th head coach at Penn State.*

1966 *The Lions beat Maryland 15-7 in Paterno's first game on their way to a 5-5 record, one of only six non-winning marks during his tenure.*

1968 *A thrilling 15-14 win over Kansas in the Orange Bowl gives Penn State an 11-0 record and No. 2 finish nationally.*

1969 *Paterno's Lions complete their second straight unbeaten campaign, but finish second again after President Nixon proclaims Texas national champions.*

1971 *Paterno calls Penn State's 30-6 win over Texas in the Cotton Bowl "one of the greatest victories in school history."*

1973 *Behind Heisman Trophy winner John Cappelletti, Penn State finishes 12-0, the third unbeaten record under Paterno.*

1976 *A 41-20 win over NC State on November 6 gives Paterno his 100th career win.*

1979 *A New Year's Day goal-line stand by Alabama denies Penn State its first national title in a 14-7 Sugar Bowl loss.*

1982 *Paterno gets a victory ride he'll remember forever following Penn State's 27-23 win over Georgia in the Sugar Bowl giving the Lions their first-ever national championship.*

1985 *Penn State enjoys another unbeaten regular season and No. 1 ranking before falling 25-10 to Oklahoma in the Orange Bowl.*

1986 *Paterno is named* Sports Illustrated *Sportsman of the Year, and AFCA Coach of the Year for the fourth time.*

1987 *Heavy underdogs to the top-ranked Miami Hurricanes, Penn State intercepts Vinny Testaverde five times in a 14-10 stunner on January 2, giving the Lions their second national title.*

1987 *Paterno earns his 200th career win in Penn State's 45-19 victory over Bowling Green on September 5.*

1990 *Paterno's 25th season as head coach is highlighted by a 24-21 win over top-ranked Notre Dame on November 17.*

1991 *Paterno becomes the first active college coach to receive the National Football Foundation and College Football Hall of Fame "Distinguished American Award."*

1993 *In its first game as a member of the Big Ten, Penn State beats Minnesota on September 4 in Beaver Stadium.*

1994 *The Lions erase a 21-0 deficit to beat Illinois 35-31 and clinch their first Big Ten title.*

1994 *Paterno becomes the first coach to win all four major bowls, as well as the winningest bowl coach, as the Lions cap a 12-0 season with a 38-20 Rose Bowl win over Oregon.*

1997 *A 30-27 win at Northwestern is Penn State's 400th since Paterno joined the staff in 1950.*

1998 *Paterno becomes the fifth coach in NCAA history to win 300 games with a 48-3 win over Bowling Green.*

2001 *A thrilling 29-27 win over Ohio State gives Paterno his 324th career win, moving him past Bear Bryant into first place on the Division I-A list.*

2003 *Paterno's image appears on a Wheaties box.*

2005 *The Nittany Lions win at least 10 games under Paterno in a fifth decade, and he is consensus national Coach of the Year after a 11-1 season. Paterno out-duels fellow legend Bobby Bowden in the Orange Bowl, 26-23.*

Paterno and the Lions reached the mountaintop with a 27-23 win over Georgia in the 1983 Sugar Bowl, giving Penn State its first undisputed national title.

The National Champions

Officially, Penn State has won two national championships. The first came in 1982, when the Lions defeated Georgia in the Sugar Bowl. The second came four years later in a Fiesta Bowl thriller over Miami that remains one of college football's biggest upsets.

But in the minds of many Nittany Lion followers, Joe Paterno's team has won at least two additional titles, possibly three. "I coached three undefeated, untied teams, and one of them won 22 games in a row," Paterno told *The Pittsburgh Press* in 1983. "They were champions as far as I was concerned. I didn't care what the country thought."

Paterno would go on to coach another unbeaten team in 1994. That squad would also have to settle for second place. The only sanctioning body that favored Penn State over Nebraska that year was Paterno's hometown newspaper, *The New York Times*.

Let the record show, however, that on two occasions there was no dispute over Penn State's reign as the best team in the country.

OK, maybe a little.

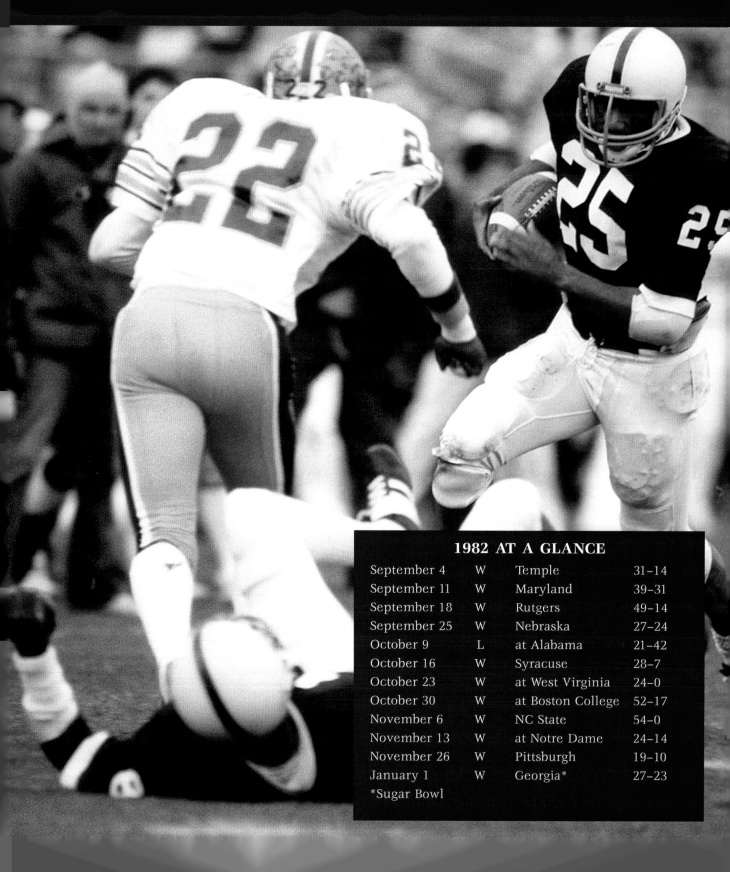

1982 AT A GLANCE

September 4	W	Temple	31–14
September 11	W	Maryland	39–31
September 18	W	Rutgers	49–14
September 25	W	Nebraska	27–24
October 9	L	at Alabama	21–42
October 16	W	Syracuse	28–7
October 23	W	at West Virginia	24–0
October 30	W	at Boston College	52–17
November 6	W	NC State	54–0
November 13	W	at Notre Dame	24–14
November 26	W	Pittsburgh	19–10
January 1	W	Georgia*	27–23

*Sugar Bowl

1982

One of the great ironies of Penn State's first national championship season is that the Nittany Lions did not finish undefeated. They had enjoyed three unbeaten seasons in the first eight years of Joe Paterno's reign and had finished no higher than second in the polls. In 1973, they tore through their season with ease, giving up a total of 32 points in their first six games and handing the ball to eventual Heisman Trophy winner John Cappelletti at the end of the season in a show of staggering offensive power. Their reward: a No. 5 ranking in the final AP and UPI rankings. Suffice it to say, Eastern football didn't get a lot of respect in back those days. And while Paterno insisted it didn't bother him, many Penn State followers weren't so nonchalant. They were starting to take it personally.

Which is one reason why the team's triumph in 1982 felt so satisfying. The Nittany Lions stuck it to the college football establishment at nearly every turn that year. They answered many of the doubts about their legitimacy by defeating the Big Eight's standard-bearer, Nebraska, 27–24, in the fourth week of the season. They quieted their Eastern rivals one by one, with a 19–10 victory over Pitt serving as the capstone to their regular season. And for the coup de grace, they defeated Herschel Walker and top-ranked Georgia in the Sugar Bowl, 27–23, to win over the South, long a bastion of Southeastern Conference solidarity.

Those victories gave Paterno the one accomplishment that had eluded him throughout his career—a national title, a rarity for an Eastern team. He got to experience the sensation of riding off the field on the shoulders of his players, a moment that will forever be engrained in the iconography of Penn State football. And he was finally able to refute the charge that he couldn't win the big one.

Which is not to say he was starved for the validation that comes with such a prestigious trophy. "I never cared that much about championships," Paterno said after the game, "except as they affected the young men who played on those teams. I was always satisfied when we won football games. That was our purpose in the sport."

The Lions won that year with a marvelous offense and a defense that was stout when it needed to be. With its wealth of skill position talent, the offense captured everyone's imagination. Todd Blackledge was a smart, resourceful quarterback, a Phi Beta Kappa no less, and he had a wealth of sure-handed receivers helping him led by Kenny Jackson and Gregg Garrity. Curt Warner was one of the best tailbacks in school history, a shifty runner with dazzling speed, and Jon Williams was much more than just a dependable backup; the Lions often used split-back formations to get both on the field at the same time.

As for the defense, it wasn't one of Penn State's all-time best, but there was no shortage of talent. Ball-hawking safety Mark

Curt Warner and the Lions gutted out a tough 19–10 win over archrival Pitt to earn a berth in the Sugar Bowl.

Robinson and linebacker Walker Lee Ashley were the stars. With two kicking specialists also returning, the Lions appeared to have the makings of a top-10 team, possibly a championship team.

Or so they thought. After four consecutive victories to open the season, things started going awry. Coming off the controversial victory over the second-ranked Cornhuskers, in which tight end Mike McCloskey appeared to be out of bounds on a 15-yard reception that set up the winning touchdown, the Lions ventured to Legion Field to face Alabama. Other than landing successfully in Birmingham, their trip was a fiasco.

The Lions had moved from eighth to third after defeating Nebraska. Alabama was ranked fourth. It was to be another momentous clash between Paterno and his old nemesis, Bear Bryant. And through the better part of four quarters, the game was fairly competitive as Penn State rebounded smartly from a 21–7 halftime deficit. Then, with five minutes to play, the Lions came unraveled. They were trailing, 27–21, when reserve Mike Suter drifted into Ralph Giacomorro and inadvertently blocked Giacomorro's punt, giving Alabama possession at the Penn State 12-yard line. The Crimson Tide scored two plays later and added another touchdown on an interception return for a 42–21 victory. It was a sudden and disastrous turn of events.

The Lions trudged to the locker room knowing they had blown a chance to state their case as potential champions. Players looked glum as they filed into the tunnel. Only when backup tailback Joel Coles got up

to speak did the mood start to lift. As historian Lou Prato recounts in his *Penn State Football Encyclopedia,* Coles gave the squad an impassioned pep talk in the locker room. He told his teammates they had six games in which to prove to the nation they were a good football team. Those words struck a chord. "You could just see a dark cloud of discouragement explode and disintegrate," Paterno wrote years later in his autobiography, *Paterno By the Book*. "The kids began to cheer for themselves."

They never stopped. The Lions won their next four games by an average margin of 34 points. After that, they got past 13th-ranked Notre Dame in frigid South Bend, 24–14, pulling away in the fourth quarter on a 48-yard touchdown pass from Blackledge to Warner.

Suddenly, they were contenders again. They had tumbled to eighth after their loss to Alabama, but with five consecutive victories they found themselves at No. 2, their highest ranking of the season.

There was one regular-season game to go. The Lions had to face fifth-ranked Pitt at home. It was a cold, blustery afternoon in State College, and neither team could develop much momentum on offense. Pitt took an early 7–3 lead and held it until the third quarter. Aided by the wind, the Lions worked with a short field and scored on a 31-yard touchdown pass from Blackledge to Jackson and a 31-yard Nick Gancitano field goal. Gancitano added field goals of 19 and 29 yards in the fourth quarter, and the defense held Pitt to a field goal after allowing the Panthers to drive to the 1-yard line.

The Lions had cleared the final hurdle. For the second time in five seasons, they would play for the national championship.

Paterno blamed Pitt's troubles in the third quarter on the weather. The Lions were used to Beaver Stadium's bluster, he said. And just to make sure, he had the kickers, quarterbacks and receivers practice outdoors a few days before the game when the wind was howling.

The weather would not be an issue in Penn State's next game. The Sugar Bowl was to be played in the climate-controlled confines of the Louisiana Superdome, a circumstance that, contrary to popular opinion, probably favored the Lions and their deep pool of playmakers.

Still, Paterno was nervous before the game, his first trip to New Orleans since the Lions' 14–7 loss to Alabama in the 1978 championship game. He paced the locker room, concerned about what Walker, the Heisman Trophy winner, might do to his defense.

He need not have worried. The Lions' defense didn't flinch. Using a variety of fronts, including an alignment with only two down linemen, Penn State scrambled the Bulldogs' blocking schemes and held Walker to 22 yards in the decisive second half (107 on 28 carries for the game).

Meanwhile, Blackledge, Warner and company were enjoying their usual success. Penn State built a 20–3 lead in the second quarter and all but clinched the victory on a 47-yard touchdown catch by Garrity in the fourth quarter.

When it was all over, Penn State players and fans jabbed their index fingers toward the roof of the Superdome and exulted, the first outburst of revelry in what was to be a long night along Bourbon Street. "This is the greatest team I've ever played on," Blackledge told the press. "It has so much character, poise and love for each other. After the loss to Alabama, we just wanted to go out and win every game one at a time. Praise the Lord, this is the greatest season I've ever had."

As satisfying as it was, the victory over Georgia put Paterno in an awkward position. Embittered by the snubs his team had received earlier in his career, he had become a staunch advocate of a Division I-A playoff. As it happened, there was another team that some believed had a claim on the 1982 national title. SMU had finished the regular season unbeaten that year behind the great running of Eric Dickerson and Craig James, the famed "Pony Express" backfield. The Mustangs were the only unbeaten team left in the country after the bowls.

But they had settled for a tie in their regular-season finale against Arkansas and were unimpressive in a 7–3 victory over Pitt in the Cotton Bowl. So while a handful of poll holdouts thought SMU deserved the title, the vast majority favored Penn State. For once, Paterno wasn't going to question their acumen. His disdain for the politicking and regional biases of the poll system were well-documented, but he finally had the upper hand. Asked by *Sports Illustrated* in the aftermath of the Sugar Bowl about his previous stance, he dismissed the question out of hand.

"Next year, let there be a playoff," he said. "This year, let's vote."

*After a 14-10 Fiesta Bowl win over Miami that nobody saw coming except for
Paterno and his team, the coach got the ride of his life from his exultant players.*

1986

Amid the ball caps and blue-and-white beer mugs that filled seemingly every storefront on College Avenue in the late 1980s was a light blue T-shirt with a disarmingly morbid theme. It depicted a "Heisman Graveyard" complete with headstones bearing the names of the many trophy winners who had been dispatched—metaphorically—by Penn State.

The shirt may not have been in good taste, but it neatly summed up the Nittany Lions' no-frills football philosophy. This was a program without an ego. The Lions didn't take pride in transforming ordinary players into superstars as so many others strived to do; to the contrary, they reveled in turning superstars into ordinary players. Penn State players had to do without the perks that their rivals enjoyed. They didn't even get to see their names on the backs of their jerseys. But from time to time they did get to take their high-profile opponents down a peg, and that sensation was even better than celebrity.

Maybe that's why the Lions' 1986 national championship resonates so deeply, even after 20 years. This was a team composed largely of overachievers, few of whom were destined for lengthy NFL careers. It boasted less star power than several of its opponents and was certainly less renowned than the 1982 national championship team.

But when it found itself up against what amounted to a future Pro Bowl team, it didn't back down. Its 14–10 victory over No. 1 Miami in the Fiesta Bowl capped Penn State's centennial season with the quintessential Penn State moment. If the Nittany Lions play football for another 100 years, there will probably never be another one quite like it. At the very least, there will never be a more notable headstone in the Heisman Graveyard than the one bearing the name of Hurricanes quarterback Vinny Testaverde.

The 1986 Nittany Lions fit Paterno's template for football success. He had never been comfortable with the 1982 team's reliance on the big play, fearing that a rip-roaring offense would commit too many turnovers. The 1986 team didn't have the players to attempt high-risk game plans. Led by quarterback John Shaffer and tailback D.J. Dozier, both experienced seniors, the offense was designed to nibble away at opponents on the ground, controlling the ball and letting the defense handle the rest. The team's leading receiver that year was Dozier with 26 catches. Its second-leading receiver was tight end Brian Siverling with 21. Its most productive wide receiver was Eric Hamilton with 19.

The Lions could get away with such conservative tactics because their defense was terrific. Indeed, it's not entirely fair to describe them as a no-name team, because they did have a star in All-America linebacker Shane Conlan, who passed up a chance to turn pro after his junior season in hopes of contending for the national championship as a senior. The players around him were solid if not as well-known. Fellow linebackers Don Graham, Pete Giftopoulos and Trey Bauer were experienced veterans who had starred on the 1985 team, which lost the national championship to Oklahoma in the Orange Bowl. Ray Isom was a big hitter at safety, and Duffy Cobbs was a tenacious cornerback. All told, it was one of the best defenses Paterno had ever assembled.

Yet for all their experience, the Lions were an unpredictable bunch. Sometimes they romped, as they did in a 23–3 road victory against second-ranked Alabama, a win that vaulted them into serious title contention.

But just as often they struggled. Their title hopes nearly disappeared in a home game against unranked Cincinnati. The Lions trailed, 17–14, with just under six minutes left to play. Faced with a third-and-10 at their own 25-yard line, they had to do what they went into the season hoping to avoid: attempt a pass downfield with the game's outcome hanging in the balance. Shaffer dropped back and had his choice of receivers. He threw to Blair Thomas, a sophomore tailback who was backing up Dozier. Thomas held on for a 32-yard gain.

After that, the outcome seemed a given. The Lions marched downfield, scoring the winning touchdown on a 6-yard run by David Clark with 3:07 left. When Conlan blocked a punt for a safety, making the final score 23–17, a wave of relief swept over the Penn State sideline. "We didn't play well," Paterno said, "But we played tough when we had to."

The same could be said of the Lions after their harrowing 17–15 victory over visiting Maryland a month later. The circumstances were similar. The offense wasn't clicking and the defense was on its heels for much of the rainy afternoon. The game's highlight came when Penn State defensive tackle Pete Curkendall intercepted a pass and began lumbering upfield. The 260-pound Curkendall picked up a convoy of blockers along the way, most of whom had to slow down to avoid getting too far ahead of him. By the time he was brought down, he had covered 82 yards. It was the longest interception return in school history that did not yield points, but the offense took care of that. Dozier scored from 9 yards out on the very next play.

Even so, Penn State nearly blew it. Leading, 17–9, with 1 minute, 4 seconds to play, the Lions allowed Maryland to score on a 27-yard touchdown pass from Dan Henning to John Bonato. There were 17 seconds left and the Terrapins trailed by only two points. With a chance to tie the score on a two-point conversion, Henning rolled out and saw James Milling in the end zone. Penn State fans looked on in horror as Milling went for the ball, but just then a lunging Cobbs tapped it away. The dream was still alive.

Penn State edged Notre Dame in South Bend, 24–19, a week later and thumped Pitt, 34–14, to close out an unbeaten regular season. With the Lions ranked second behind Miami, there was no choice but to put the two major independents together in the Fiesta Bowl, the only major bowl game unencumbered by a conference tie-in. Was this a must-see matchup? Some weren't sure. Penn State was playing for No. 1 for the second time in as many years, but as Prato notes in his *Penn State Football Encyclopedia,* players felt the public wasn't giving them their due. As Bauer told reporters at the time, "We're still that big, slow team with no talent wearing the black shoes but playing again for the national championship."

The Nittany Lions didn't have a fraction of Miami's star power. Testaverde had just won the Heisman Trophy and his

receivers—Michael Irvin, Brett Perriman and Brian Blades—were superb, as was tailback Alonzo Highsmith. On defense, the Hurricanes were led by the incomparable Jerome Brown, a one-man mob scene who blew up plays with abandon from his tackle post.

The Nittany Lions' only chance, it seemed, was to force Miami into making turnovers, get a big play or two from the offense and hope for the best.

Which is exactly what happened. Though thoroughly outgained by Testaverde and company, the Lions took a 14–10 lead on a 6-yard Dozier touchdown run with eight minutes left. Conlan, playing on a gimpy knee, had set up the score by returning an interception 39 yards.

When the Hurricanes finally got into a rhythm on their last drive, it didn't last long. Faced with a fourth-and-goal at the Penn State 13-yard line, Testaverde dropped back and scanned the field. There were nine seconds left. He could have run for an easy touchdown because the Lions had dropped their linebackers into coverage. Instead, he lobbed a pass toward Perriman and watched as Giftopoulos stepped in front of it to end the threat. It was the last pass of Testaverde's college career, and possibly the worst. Said Giftopoulos, "Any one of four players could have intercepted it or knocked it down."

And with that, the celebration in the desert began. Players hoisted Paterno on their shoulders and carried him off the field, a scene reminiscent of his victory ride

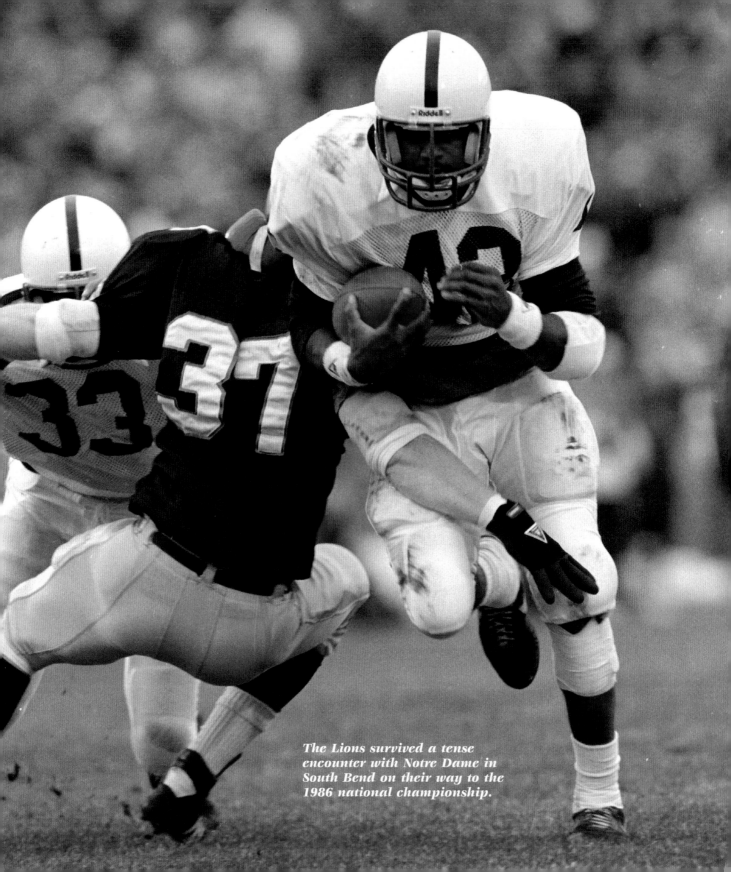

The Lions survived a tense encounter with Notre Dame in South Bend on their way to the 1986 national championship.

following the Sugar Bowl five years earlier. The Lions' strategy had worked. They had intercepted Testaverde five times, thwarting an offense that had once seemed unstoppable. "I think everything happened that you hope would happen," Paterno said, "Particularly since this is our 100th year and we had a bunch of kids that worked hard to make it happen. Sometimes people work hard and it doesn't happen."

Other than the game itself, the encounter between Miami and Penn State went as expected, including the postscript. The Hurricanes' stars moved on to NFL. Testaverde played 20 seasons and attended two Pro Bowls. Irvin played 11 years and went to five Pro Bowls. Perriman, Highsmith and Blades all enjoyed long pro careers. Brown became a star with the Philadelphia Eagles, making two Pro Bowls in five seasons before being killed in a traffic accident in 1992. His number was later retired by the team.

The Nittany Lions didn't make quite the same splash. The only starters from the 1986 national championship team to enjoy prolonged NFL success were Conlan, offensive tackle Steve Wisniewski, defensive tackle Tim Johnson and fullback Steve Smith. Other players didn't pan out, most notably Dozier, a first-round draft pick who gave up the sport after five seasons to try baseball. Most others simply got on with their life's work.

Giftopoulos, the hero of Penn State's final goal-line stand, embodied its low-key approach to the game. While Testaverde and Perriman were starring in the NFL, the Ontario native was plugging away in the Canadian Football League. He never did attain international renown, and when asked about the one fleeting moment in which he was the biggest star in football, he downplayed his role.

"I just happened to be in the right place at the right time," he said. "The biggest thing was winning the national championship."

1986 AT A GLANCE			
September 6	W	Temple	45–15
September 20	W	at Boston College	26–14
September 27	W	East Carolina	42–17
October 4	W	Rutgers	31–6
October 11	W	Cincinnati	23–17
October 18	W	Syracuse	42–3
October 25	W	at Alabama	23–3
November 1	W	at West Virginia	19–0
November 8	W	Maryland	17–15
November 15	W	at Notre Dame	24–19
November 22	W	Pittsburgh	34–14
January 2	W	Miami*	14–10
*Fiesta Bowl			

The 1994 Penn State offense, led by quarterback Kerry Collins,
was one of the greatest in college football history.

Nittany Lion Superlatives

Penn State football history is littered with moments of greatness—national championships won, great games played, superior individual efforts, memorable upsets and more. Here is a small sample of that record of achievement.

THE GREATEST GAMES

This section could go on forever. Penn State has played some of college football's most memorable games. Its victory over Miami in the 1987 Fiesta Bowl remains the most watched college football game in history. Seventy million viewers tuned in to see the Nittany Lions play the Hurricanes for the national championship in the 1987 Fiesta Bowl.

The Lions haven't played for any more titles since that night in Tempe, but they've been involved in their share of big games through the years. Here's a look at some of the biggest.

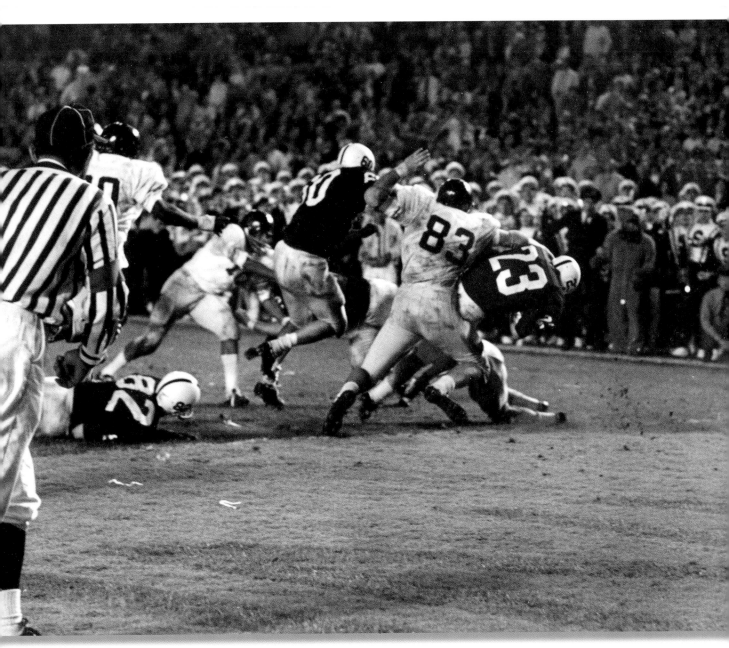

The stunning comeback win over Kansas in the Orange Bowl capped an unbeaten season.

1969 ORANGE BOWL
Penn State 15, Kansas 14

Penn State's 1968 season is still spoken of in hushed, reverent tones. This was the year in which the Nittany Lions put it all together, establishing themselves not just as the East's premiere program but as a force on the national scene. It was Paterno's first unbeaten season, and it was also the season in which his first batch of great players—Charlie Pittman, Ted Kwalick, Dennis Onkotz, Steve Smear and Mike Reid, among others—all came of age.

It's easy, in retrospect, to look back on the 1968 season as a *fait accompli*. In reality, it took a near miracle for the Lions to enjoy a happy ending.

No. 3 Penn State trailed sixth-ranked Kansas, 14–7, with 1 minute, 16 seconds to play. But after struggling against the Jayhawks' defense all night, Chuck Burkhart completed a 45-yard pass to Bobby Campbell at the 3-yard line. Three plays later, Burkhart rolled left on a keeper and barreled into the end zone.

Penn State still trailed by a point. Paterno wasn't interested in settling for a tie, so he had Burkhart roll out again. This time the Lions weren't so fortunate. The quarterback's pass to Kwalick was high, and Kansas fans climbed over the railing at the Orange Bowl and swarmed the field. It was pandemonium until everyone noticed the flag lying on the goal line.

It turned out Kansas had had 12 men on the field. The play had to be run again, this time from the 2-yard line. Given the unlikeliest of reprieves, the Lions made good. They ran a sweep with Campbell sprinting to his left and lunging over the goal line. Final score: Penn State 15, Kansas 14.

These days, State's victory is viewed as a stepping-stone, a young coach's first tentative step on the road to immortality. But in the immediate aftermath of the game, Nittany Lion players did not feel as though they had been swept up in destiny's embrace. "To be honest," Reid told *The Pittsburgh Press*, "I don't know how we won this one."

PENN STATE 48, PITT 14

November 28, 1981

Few games in Penn State history have done more for blue-and-white self-esteem than this one. To this day, Penn State fans can end any argument with Pitt boosters by reciting the words "forty-eight–fourteen." It's the nuclear option, a rhetorical device so devastating that no rebuttal is possible. How could there be? Pitt went into the game unbeaten, ranked No. 1 and sporting a future NFL Hall of Famer at quarterback. It came out with its national championship hopes in tatters.

Which is not to say that Pitt didn't have its moments. It did. But they were compressed into a flawless first quarter, in which Dan Marino completed 9-of-10 passes and guided the Panthers to two easy touchdowns.

After that, it was all Penn State. Roger Jackson intercepted Marino in the end zone with the Panthers poised to take a 21–0 lead, and the Lions' whiplash comeback was under way. Later in the second quarter, Mike Meade plunged into the opposite end zone for the first of 48 unanswered points. The rout was on.

In the end, the Nittany Lions got great performances from just about everybody. They got 262 passing yards from Todd Blackledge and 104 rushing yards from Curt Warner. Receiver Kenny Jackson, who had caught only 14 passes in the first 10 games of the regular season, had five receptions for 158 yards and two touchdowns.

The cumulative effect of those efforts was to humble a Pitt team that had designs on the national championship. "Give Penn State credit," tight end John Brown told *The Pittsburgh Press.* "They deserved to win."

1983 SUGAR BOWL

Penn State 27, Georgia 23

The play was called "6–43." Four players would fan out at the line of scrimmage and streak down the field, receivers Kenny Jackson and Gregg Garrity on the outside, tailback Curt Warner and tight end Mike McCloskey on the hash marks.

When the Lions ran the play in the regular season, they usually threw to Jackson, their speedy All-American. But with the fourth quarter under way and Penn State clinging to a 20–17 lead over No. 1 Georgia, quarterback Todd Blackledge went in a different direction. He went to Garrity.

Garrity? A few years earlier, this young prospect would never have struck anyone as a potential Sugar Bowl hero. He was planning to attend Kent State, where he would have played for Blackledge's father, Ron. But Kent declined to offer him a scholarship, so he decided to walk on at Penn State. Once on campus, he impressed the coaches with his sure hands and workaholic demeanor. He eventually earned a starting position on a team that boasted one of the best offenses in school history.

As Blackledge's pass began fluttering back down to earth, Garrity could see it was slightly overthrown. He sprawled out in the end zone, straddling the left sideline, and caught it for a

47-yard touchdown. There was still nearly a quarter to play, but the catch gave Penn State a 27–17 lead and took some of the fight out of Georgia.

Garrity ended the game with four receptions for 116 yards. Thanks to his performance, as well as strong efforts from Blackledge (223 passing yards), Warner (117 rushing yards) and a rugged defense, the Nittany Lions were able to hold off the favored Bulldogs and claim their first national championship.

Garrity ended up on the cover of *Sports Illustrated.* The shot of him holding the ball aloft in celebration is one of Penn State's iconic images. Go to any bar or bookstore in downtown State College and you'll see it hanging on a wall somewhere. Penn State fans will always remember that moment, and they will always remember Garrity.

"Everyone always asks me what my best catch was," he once told *Blue White Illustrated.* "I don't even have to answer that most of the time, because people will just answer it for me. It's probably one of the more important catches. I don't know if it's actually my best catch, but it's definitely one of the ones that I will most remember."

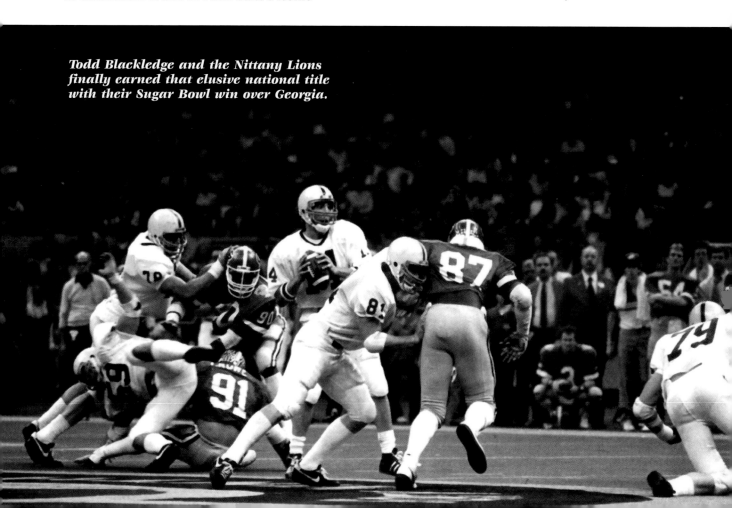

Todd Blackledge and the Nittany Lions finally earned that elusive national title with their Sugar Bowl win over Georgia.

1987
FIESTA BOWL
Penn State 14, Miami 10

The run-up to Penn State's third national championship game in five years was laughably hyperbolic. Miami players dis-embarked from their plane wearing combat fatigues and running their mouths. Penn State players showed in Tempe wearing blazers and ties. Thus the theme of teams' stay in the Arizona desert was set. This was to be the white hats vs. the black hats. Rebel alliance vs. galactic empire. Good vs. evil.

The pregame lunacy reached a cre-scendo at a steak dinner attended by both teams. Offended by one of Penn State punter John Bruno's remarks, Miami defensive tackle Jerome Brown led his teammates back to their bus. "Did the Japanese sit down and have dinner with Pearl Harbor before they bombed them?" he asked. Well, no, they didn't. So out the Hurricanes went. But Bruno would have the last word. As Miami players were filing out of the tent, he grabbed a microphone. "Excuse me," he said, "but didn't the Japanese lose?"

Brown's unfortunate metaphor turned out to be the first of many mis-takes. After a week of Category 5 trash talk, the Hurricanes failed to back up any of their bluster. Penn State down-graded the 'Canes' potent offense using a clever scheme masterminded by defen-sive coordinator Jerry Sandusky. Instead of putting pressure on quarterback

Vinny Testaverde, the Lions sat back in the passing lanes, punished Miami's receivers with a succession of big hits and waited for Testaverde to start making mistakes. They didn't wait long.

Testaverde, who had just won the Heisman Trophy, threw five intercep-tions in his final college game. The fourth of those errant passes was picked off by Shane Conlan to set up a 6-yard touchdown run by D.J. Dozier that put the Lions ahead midway through the fourth quarter. It was their first lead of the game.

Testaverde's fifth interception came at an even less opportune moment. Facing fourth-and-goal from the Penn State 13-yard line, he looked for Brett Perriman in the end zone. Instead he found Pete Giftopoulos. The junior line-backer stepped in front of Testaverde's pass and into immortality. Penn State took possession and ran out the final 18 seconds of the game for its second national championship.

With that, the pregame silliness finally receded. The combat fatigues, the steak fry incident, the hype—none of it mattered. All that mattered was that Penn State had held on. Linebacker Trey Bauer, one of the few Nittany Lions willing to fire back at Miami's trash talkers, had a fitting final analysis. "Everybody just sucked it up," he said. "We couldn't lose."

An inspired Nittany Lion defense harassed Heisman Trophy winner
Vinny Testaverde into a five-interception nightmare.

PENN STATE 35, ILLINOIS 31
November 12, 1994

It could have ended in tears. Instead, it ended in triumph. Penn State's comeback victory over the Fighting Illini is probably remembered more fondly than any other game from the team's undefeated 1994 season, including its historic Rose Bowl triumph over Oregon. An argument can be made that it's Penn State's greatest victory since joining the Big Ten.

Going in, no one expected such a dramatic game. Penn State was ranked second, while unranked Illinois had already lost three games. But Penn State was having a terrible trip to Champaign. The Lions' hotel had lost power the morning of the game, and everyone's routine was a little off. For their pregame meal, players dined on takeout pizza. Then came kickoff, and things really started to go downhill.

The Illini roared to a 21–0 lead in the first quarter. Penn State's powerful offense couldn't get into a rhythm. Kerry Collins threw eight consecutive incompletions at one point, and nobody else was able to get untracked.

But this offense was too good to go dark for 60 minutes. The Lions began creeping back in the second quarter and trailed 28–14 at halftime. By the fourth quarter, they had shaved Illinois' lead to a field goal, 31–28. The wind and rain were picking up. When the Lions took possession at their own 4-yard line with 6 minutes, 7 seconds to play, the field conditions were inhospitable. It

didn't matter. Collins calmly guided Penn State to the Illinois 2-yard line. On first-and-goal, he stuffed the ball into the gut of fullback Brian Milne and watched as Milne followed blockers Jeff Hartings, Keith Olsommer and Jason Sload into the end zone for the winning touchdown. It was an unforgettable moment.

A few hours later, the team was back in State College, still unbeaten, still harboring national championship hopes. Paterno and his players appeared at an impromptu pep rally in Rec Hall and celebrated with their fans. They had every reason to exult. "We never quit," Collins said. "We never gave up."

1995 ROSE BOWL
Penn State 38, Oregon 20

This game was a microcosm of Penn State's bittersweet 1994 season. The offense was terrific, the defense erratic and the pollsters indifferent.

Playing in their first Rose Bowl since 1923, the Nittany Lions won handily, but they didn't come away with the grand prize. They weren't able to seize a piece of the 1994 national championship, a title that some said—and still say—they deserved.

As far as the polls were concerned, the Lions' fate was sealed when No. 1 Nebraska rallied to defeat Miami in the Orange Bowl the night before. Some players reported that they heard furniture crashing in adjoining hotel rooms as the Cornhuskers launched their comeback. Everyone understood the situation: Nebraska coach Tom Osborne was a sentimental favorite, and a victory over 12th-ranked Oregon, no matter how lopsided, wasn't going to sway enough voters to make a difference.

Still, the Nittany Lions came out focused. Ki-Jana Carter blasted through a hole on Penn State's first play from scrimmage and charged 81 yards for a touchdown. Penn State scored again on a Brian Milne touchdown plunge late in the second quarter. And while Oregon kept counterpunching thanks to the deft passing of Danny O'Neil, who finished with 456 yards, the Ducks couldn't keep it up. The Lions pulled ahead, 28–14, in the third quarter on Carter's third touchdown run of the game. He would go on to rush for 156 yards in his final college game, and the Lions wouldn't have to sweat out the final quarter.

"We're worthy of being considered national champions like anyone else," Paterno said afterward in a crowded media room. Penn State fans agreed. To bolster their case, they cited the 1991 season, in which Miami and Washington split the title. They also cited the 1990 season, in which Colorado and Georgia Tech shared the crown even though the Buffaloes' 11–1–1 record was tainted because of the infamous "fifth down" officiating fiasco.

It didn't matter. When the polls came out, Nebraska was atop both. The Lions had to settle for No. 2. It was the fourth time a Paterno-coached team had finished unbeaten only to see the pollsters declare someone else champion.

Ki-Jana Carter found paydirt three times in the Rose Bowl rout of the Ducks.

PENN STATE 29, OHIO STATE 27
October 27, 2001

Nobody expected Joe Paterno's pursuit of the all-time coaching victories record to run into October. Nobody expected it to extend into 2001, for that matter. But the Nittany Lions were a mess in the early 2000s, soft on defense and dreadful on offense, and things tended to get away from them.

Which is why their victory over Ohio State was such a giddy thrill. For once, everything clicked. Behind and passing and running of redshirt freshman quarterback Zack Mills, Penn State finally showed it could compete against one of the Big Ten's traditional powers. Replacing beleaguered starter Matt Senneca after just one series, Mills put a charge in Penn State's offense. His 69-yard sprint on an option play reignited the team after it fell behind by 18 points in the third quarter. Penn State scored 20 unanswered points to end the game. Eric McCoo scored the winning touchdown on a 14-yard pass from Mills early in the fourth quarter.

But if the game itself was Mills' stage—he passed for 280 yards and rushed for 138—the aftermath was Paterno's. Players carried him around the field on their shoulders following his 324th victory, the one that moved him past Bear Bryant and made him the winningest major-college football coach in history. They snapped photos and presented him with a ring to commemorate the milestone.

Paterno instinctively tried to turn the spotlight back on his players. "I can't tell you how proud I am of this football team," he said from atop a makeshift podium in the middle of the field. "They could have packed it in a long time ago." But the players wanted no part of it. This was Joe's show. In the locker room after the game they cried as he spoke.

The Lions would go on to finish 5–6 for their second consecutive losing season. The victory over the Buckeyes would prove to be a bright spot in a bleak period. But it was extraordinarily bright. Said defensive tackle Jimmy Kennedy, "I'm happy the old man got it. He deserves it."

Michael Robinson and the Lions gutted out an Orange Bowl win over Florida State.

2006
ORANGE BOWL
Penn State 26, Florida State 23

Joe Paterno couldn't have seemed less enthused about Penn State's first appearance in the Bowl Championship Series. The 79-year-old coach was gruff and ornery in the weeks leading up to the game. He cut off the moderator of an Orange Bowl news conference in mid-sentence, grumbled about his media obligations and pined for the good old days when coaches and their bowl committee friends made backroom deals to decide who went where. A few days before the game, he spelled it all out. "I need another big game like I need a hole in the head," he said.

But Penn State did need another big game. After four losing seasons in five years, the Nittany Lions needed the validation they were sure to get with an Orange Bowl victory over Bobby Bowden's high-profile Seminoles. And in the end, they did get it, but by the slimmest of margins.

Penn State squandered its chance to win the game in regulation, as Kevin Kelly missed a 29-yard field goal attempt with 32 seconds left. Kelly missed another potential winner at the end of the first overtime, setting up a second overtime period in which the teams traded touchdowns. For a while, it seemed neither team wanted to win. But in the third overtime, Kelly's 29-yard kick sailed through the uprights, ending the 4 hour, 45 minute marathon and giving Paterno his first postseason victory since 1999.

Afterward, Paterno and his players smiled as they filed into the postgame media room. It was well after 1 a.m., but the coach was a ray of sunshine, his dour mood having lifted with Kelly's final kick. "I'm just so pleased for these guys," he said. "They came off a couple of lousy years, got together and made up their minds that that was enough."

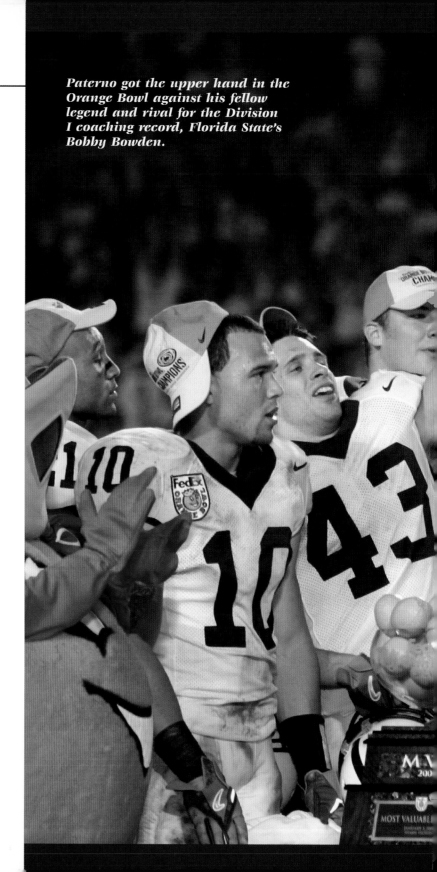

Paterno got the upper hand in the Orange Bowl against his fellow legend and rival for the Division I coaching record, Florida State's Bobby Bowden.

2007 OUTBACK BOWL
Penn State 20, Tennessee 10

No one is calling him ageless anymore, but Joe Paterno still knows how to get his team ready to play bowl games. With the 80-year-old coach watching from the press box—his leg was broken in a sideline collision at Wisconsin two months earlier—Penn State defeated Tennessee, 20–10, in the 2007 Outback Bowl. It was the team's eighth victory in its past 10 bowl games and the 22nd postseason victory of Paterno's career.

"I was hoping we would play with a lot of poise and that we would hustle all the time and that the young kids, when they got in there, would carry their load," Paterno said. "I think all of those things happened."

Tony Hunt rushed for 158 yards on a career-high 31 carries in his final college game to lift the Nittany Lions past the then-17th-ranked Volunteers. But it was another Tony—sophomore cornerback Tony Davis—who supplied the key play. With Tennessee poised to break a 10–10 tie early in the fourth quarter, Davis alertly scooped up an Arian Foster fumble and dashed 88 yards to the opposite end zone. Tennessee never recovered from the whiplash momentum shift. Penn State clamped down in the final 10 minutes, handing the ball to Hunt and watching him demolish a fatigued Vols defensive front.

The Nittany Lions improved to 9–4 with the victory and finished 24th in the final Associated Press poll. Though its season was not an unqualified success—the team had uncharacteristically lost its previous four games against ranked opponents—Penn State looked awfully familiar in its finale, giving rise to hopes that Paterno has something even more grandiose in store as he heads into the twilight of his coaching career.

Tony Hunt in the Outback Bowl, 2007.

THE GREAT TEAMS
1968–1969 Seasons

If he coaches another 41 years—and it's starting to look like a possibility—Joe Paterno will probably never figure out how these great unbeaten teams failed to win at least a piece of a national championship. Boasting a talented roster that included five future College Hall of Famers and two future Pro Football Hall of Famers, the Lions went 11–0 both years yet finished No. 2 in the Associated Press rankings.

The 1969 season, in particular, still rankles. Before the regular season ended, the third-ranked Lions turned down a Cotton Bowl invitation to face No. 2 Texas, voting instead to play Missouri in the Orange Bowl. Their rationale was twofold. First, the Lions didn't think the national title was within reach because No. 1 Ohio State was destined for the Rose Bowl. Second, some of the team's African-American players felt they would not be welcome in Texas.

So off to Miami they went. But Ohio State lost its regular-season finale to Michigan and suddenly the title was up for grabs. Texas went on to defeat Arkansas in its final regular-season game, and President Nixon, attending the game, congratulated the Longhorns in the locker room on their national championship. The pollsters followed Nixon's lead and named Texas No. 1 after its Cotton Bowl victory over Notre Dame, even though the Lions had the nation's longest winning streak after stifling Missouri in a 10–3 Orange Bowl triumph.

The president's involvement in the decision was controversial. Nixon tried to sooth angry Pennsylvanians with a plaque honoring the Lions for their 22-game winning streak. When Paterno responded with a terse thanks-but-no-thanks, Penn Staters everywhere cheered. As far as they were concerned, impeachment came four years too late.

1973 SEASON

John Cappelletti was the star of Penn State's unbeaten 1973 season. The bruising tailback rushed for 1,522 yards and 17 touchdowns and won the school's only Heisman Trophy.

Cappelletti's triumph, and especially his moving Heisman Trophy acceptance speech, overshadowed the rest of the season. The Nittany Lions' performance in 1973 is not as ingrained in Penn State lore the way the 1968 and 1969 seasons are, or the way the 1994 Rose Bowl season is, perhaps because the squad finished fifth in the polls despite going 12–0.

Penn State excelled thanks to Cappelletti and a stout defense captained by linebacker Ed O'Neil and defensive tackle Randy Crowder. Paterno called it his best team in eight seasons as Penn State's head coach. After a 16–9 victory over LSU in the Orange Bowl, it didn't appear he was exaggerating.

Except for a near upset against North Carolina State, in which Penn State

Penn State's Orange Bowl win over LSU capped the Nittany Lions' third unbeaten season in six years.

surrendered 29 points, the defense was superb all season. And when Cappelletti hit his stride with three consecutive 200-yard games late in the year, the Lions looked all but unstoppable.

The Orange Bowl showed Penn State at its resourceful best. Cappelletti wasn't effective in his final college game. Bothered by an ankle injury, and by a patch of slick artificial turf that he called "the worst surface I ever played on," he managed only 50 yards rushing. But the

defense was as stingy as ever. After the Lions allowed a first-quarter touchdown, the only points Penn State surrendered came on a safety after a botched punt attempt.

Notre Dame ended up winning the national title by upsetting Alabama in the Sugar Bowl. But Penn State players, echoing the words of their predecessors, didn't concede anything to the Irish. "I don't think they won the championship," O'Neil told *The Pittsburgh Press*. "They didn't play us."

It ended in heartbreak,
but the 1979 Sugar Bowl
was one for the ages.

1978 SEASON

The Nittany Lions were hoping this would be their break-through. The pieces were in place. Finally, they didn't have to do their usual postseason scoreboard watching. Finally, they held their destiny in their own hands.

So what happened? They lost. In one of the most disheartening defeats of the Joe Paterno era, the No. 1 Lions fell to No. 2 Alabama in the 1979 Sugar Bowl, 14–7, coming up short on fourth-and-goal when Mike Guman was stuffed for no gain on a run up the middle late in the fourth quarter.

In his autobiography, Paterno wrote that he wanted to call a pass on fourth down. He wanted Chuck Fusina to fake a handoff then look for the tight end in the end zone. But, as he went on to explain, his assistant coaches talked him out of it, believing that if the Nittany Lions couldn't gain a yard on the ground they didn't deserve the national title. Penn State couldn't get that yard as Paterno's rival, Bear Bryant, showed his team was worthier of the championship. The Lions' veteran coach didn't come out of his funk for months.

Now that the raw emotions of that night have simmered down, it's easier to assess the legacy of Penn State's 1978 team. The Lions were loaded that year, especially on defense, where stalwarts such as Matt Millen and Bruce Clark helped hold eight regular-season opponents to 10 points or fewer. They also had a heady senior quarterback in Fusina and a fine offensive line anchored by future College Football Hall of Famer Keith Dorney.

But this star-crossed team missed out on its chance at immortality by less than a yard. After reaching No. 1 for the first time in school history, it finished fourth in both polls.

Unbeaten, but unloved by the pollsters: the 1994 Nittany Lions.

1994 SEASON

Some say Penn State's 1994 offense was the best in college football history. The Nittany Lions averaged 47 points and 520 yards a game and became the first Big Ten team to enjoy a perfect season since Ohio State went 10–0 in 1968. In the process, they catapulted a number of players to stardom. Five starters on the offense would become first-round NFL draftees: Ki-Jana Carter, Kerry Collins and Kyle Brady in 1995; Jeff Hartings and Andre Johnson the following year.

The knock on Penn State—and the likely reason it didn't lay claim to Joe Paterno's third national championship—was that its defense was nothing special. It had a number of talented players, notably linebackers Terry Killens and Brian Gelzheiser and safety Kim Herring. But the Lions gave up a lot of yards, and occasionally a lot of points.

Penn State surrendered big yardage in a 35–29 victory at Indiana, a game that many view as the de facto end of Penn State's title chase. The Lions lost support in the polls because of the close score, even though the Hoosiers got their last two touchdowns in the final two minutes of the game against a defense consisting of walk-ons and backups.

Regardless, the Lions finished 12–0 and convinced themselves of their title-worthiness, if not the pollsters. "We're going to award ourselves the national championship," Collins told the *Pittsburgh Post-Gazette* following Penn State's 38–20 victory over Oregon in the Rose Bowl, "no matter what the guys in their [easy] chairs say."

2005 SEASON

Penn State's 2005 season was among the most satisfying in school history, partly because it was just the sort of season that many thought Joe Paterno didn't have in him anymore. The Lions had won a combined total of seven games the previous two years, and many were calling on the 78-year-old coach to step down. As the *Pittsburgh Post-Gazette* reported, university president Graham Spanier spearheaded an effort by several administrators to convince the veteran coach to retire following the 2004 season. Less than a year later, Spanier was helping Paterno whip a throng of Penn State zealots into a froth at an Orange Bowl pep rally in Miami. It's funny how things work out sometimes.

Of course, there was tension along the way. The Lions needed to convert a fourth-and-15 against Northwestern in the final two minutes to keep the winning touchdown drive going. A loss to the unranked Wildcats in its Big Ten opener could have shattered the team's fragile confidence. But Penn State prevailed in Evanston, 34–29. And two weeks later it rocked sixth-ranked Ohio State, 17–10, putting the program back in the national spotlight.

The Lions would remain in the spotlight for the rest of the season, finishing 11–1 and ranked third in the final polls. It was the 13th top-five finish of Paterno's career.

Matt Suhey goes airborne in 1977's Pitt-Penn State classic, won by the Lions 15–13.

The Rivalries

The trouble with evaluating Penn State's rivalries is that many of them aren't really rivalries at all, if by "rivalry" you mean an ongoing battle between competitive equals. The teams Penn State has faced most often during the Joe Paterno era—Pitt, West Virginia, Maryland, Syracuse, Rutgers and Temple—sport a collective record of 18–148–2 against the Lions' longtime coach. Worse, Penn State is now ensconced in the Big Ten. As infrequently as the Nittany Lions face those traditional opponents anymore, it will take them millennia to catch up.

Since the start of the Big Ten era in 1993, Penn State has tried to straddle a difficult line. School officials have strived to maintain a few old relationships with former Eastern compatriots while building new rivalries with the team's conference brethren. It hasn't been easy. There were hard feelings when Penn State fled the Major Independents to take up with the likes of Michigan and Ohio State. Some of those wounds may never heal.

Of course, hard feelings and old wounds are what rivalries are all about. Here's a look at some teams that Penn Staters love to hate, and vice versa.

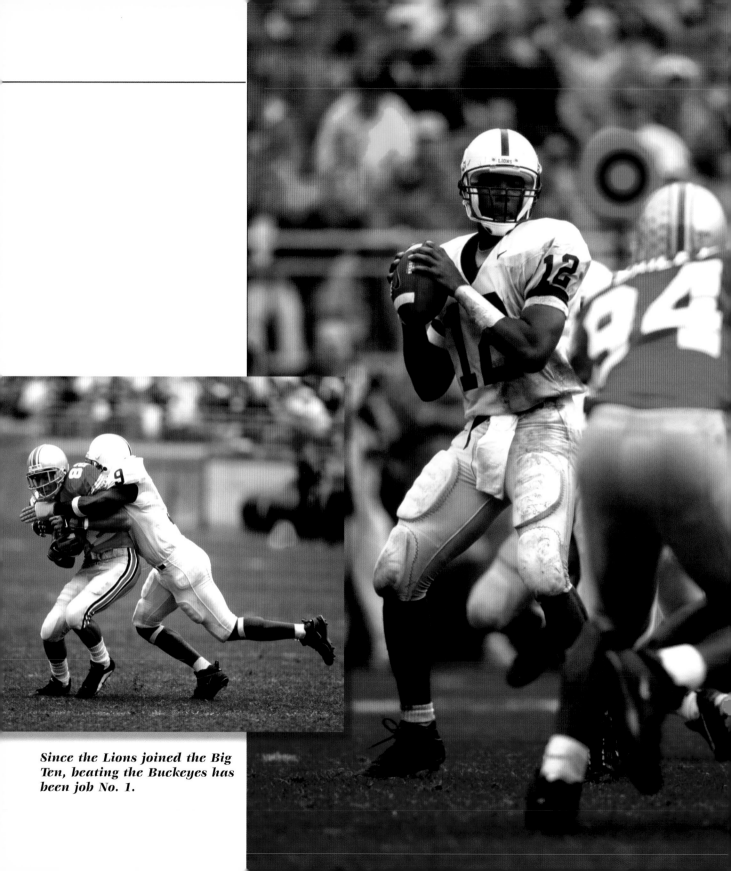

Since the Lions joined the Big Ten, beating the Buckeyes has been job No. 1.

PENN STATE VS. OHIO STATE

Of all the rivalries Penn State has forged since joining the Big Ten, this one has the most compelling backstory. The Nittany Lions and Buckeyes didn't have a rivalry per se heading into Penn State's landmark 1993 season. But they did have a history.

The two teams played eight games before becoming conference rivals. That was only natural given that they reside in adjoining states and often cross the border in pursuit of recruits.

Included in that list of games are two that still bring joy to the hearts of longtime Penn State fans. In 1978, the Lions traveled to Columbus and throttled the sixth-ranked Buckeyes, 19–0. Penn State gave true freshman quarterback Art Schlichter a merciless hazing with five interceptions and a fumble recovery.

The teams met again in the 1980 Fiesta Bowl. Schlichter was by then an experienced junior. For a while it looked as though he would have his revenge. But after falling behind, 19–7, Penn State scored 24 unanswered points and won easily, 31–19.

Since becoming conference rivals, the intensity has skyrocketed. There's some genuine bad blood between the two schools, much of it stemming from the carnival surrounding the games rather than the games themselves.

Things got off to a rocky start when Penn State suffered a 24–6 defeat in Columbus in 1993. The Lions couldn't cope with Ohio State's size advantage on the line of scrimmage and watched as Raymont Harris galloped across a sloppy field for 151 yards. The defeat came on the heels of a 21–13 loss to Michigan two weeks earlier, and it hurt having to hear critics charge that Penn State wasn't physical enough for the Big Ten. But what really galled Penn State fans was the news that Ohio State president Gordon Gee had been gloating in the press box during the game. "John Cooper out-coached Joe Paterno," Gee reportedly said. "I want you to print that."

Those words were still stuck in many Penn State craws the following year. The rematch delighted revenge-minded Nittany Lion supporters, as Penn State overwhelmed the Buckeyes, 63–14. It was Ohio State's most lopsided loss since 1946. But after the game, the top-ranked Lions actually fell to No. 2 behind Nebraska in the AP poll. Conspiracy theorists surmised that voters in Big Ten country, resentful of the Lions' presence in the conference, refused to get behind Paterno's team the way voters in other regions supported their local teams. It may or may not have been true, but it sounded true to Penn State fans. They had developed a bit of a persecution complex after the Lions were denied the No. 1 ranking following their three previous unbeaten seasons under Paterno. The 1994 season would do nothing to allay those suspicions.

There would be more drama, and more hard feelings as the series with Ohio State went on. The low point came in 2000 when a freshman defensive back named Adam Taliaferro was knocked unconscious while trying to make a tackle late in a blowout loss at Ohio Stadium. Taliaferro was taken from the field in an immobilizing stretcher as Penn State teammates held hands in prayer. When play resumed, the Lions were still in a daze. Leading, 38–6, with 1:35 to play, Ohio State broke its huddle and completed a pass on fourth-and-6 to set up one final touchdown. Many Penn State fans felt the decision to attack at that moment was unsportsmanlike and held a grudge against Cooper even after his dismissal at the end of the season.

The high point came a year later when Penn State edged the Buckeyes, 29–27, at Beaver Stadium. It was Paterno's 324th career victory, one more than Bear Bryant amassed, and it gave him the all-time major-college record. While it might not have mattered to the coach, Penn State fans were tickled to see the mark come at the expense of a heated rival.

There have been other wild happenings in this series, which is tied, 11–11. In 2003, Scott McMullen completed a 5-yard pass to Michael Jenkins with 1:35 remaining to give Ohio State a 21–20 victory at Beaver Stadium. Two years later, Penn State whipped a capacity crowd into a frenzy and defeated sixth-ranked Ohio State to re-emerge as a national power after two seasons in the wilderness.

The strangest moment of all may have happened during an otherwise forgettable 1998 game at Ohio Stadium. When the Buckeyes scored just before halftime, assistant coach Tim Salem burst from his seat in the coaches' booth and pounded on a windowpane, showering the reporters below him with broken glass. As heads turned, Salem stormed out of the box without apology. When the second half began, there was electrical tape over the places where razor-sharp shards dangled, and reporters were still picking glass out of their hair.

That's the kind of rivalry this has become. It's the kind in which there's always something interesting happening, the kind in which even the noncombatants aren't safe.

"We have had a great series," Paterno said. "It's a fun game."

PENN STATE VS. MICHIGAN

Is it still a rivalry if the same team keeps winning all the games? That's the question Penn Staters no doubt found themselves asking after Michigan defeated the Lions last October, 17–10. It was the Wolverines' eighth consecutive victory over Penn State, a streak dating to 1997. And though the result was hardly unexpected given that Michigan was ascendant in 2006, it left the Nittany Lions and their followers even more frustrated than ever. Surely this opponent can be beaten, they had to be thinking as they filed out of Beaver Stadium.

Penn State's toughest Big Ten foe: the Michigan Wolverines.

Jeff Hartings slams a Michigan lineman to the turf.

But how? No matter what the situation, the Wolverines always seem to find a way to foil their newfound nemesis—"the 11th team"—as they haughtily described Penn State on its entry into the Big Ten. They win defensive struggles. They win track meets. They shut the Lions out with their raging, frothing defensive bullies. They rally for touchdowns in the closing seconds. They prove so elusive, so slippery, that the only way to cope with their dominance is to go into denial, as Joe Paterno seemed to do when asked at a 2006 news conference about not being able to "get over the hump" against Michigan. Said the coach, "I don't even know what you are talking about, really.

"Michigan is a fine team. When you play them, you are going to be in a tough football game," he continued. "They are well-coached, have a lot of good personnel, good tradition, and they play hard. We've had a couple of tough games with them."

A couple? Try nine. The Wolverines hold a 9–3 edge in the series and they get to face the Lions at the Big House in 2007. It could take Penn State decades to catch up.

And yet even as the series grows more lopsided, it remains heated, more heated by far than Penn State's "official" rivalry against Michigan State. And it's not hard to figure out why. There's something about seeing two of college football's most historically successful programs clash that stirs emotions on both sides.

It seems hard to believe given their long histories and the relative proximity of their campuses, but Penn State and Michigan didn't play each other in football until the Nittany Lions joined the Big Ten in 1993. The schools had had little contact through the years, although Michigan athletic director Don Canham did approach Paterno about coaching the Wolverines before hiring a young firebrand named Bo Schembechler in 1968. Michigan was one of four conference teams the Lions had never faced prior to its inaugural Big Ten season. If the Wolverines' athletic brass had gotten their way, the two schools would have continued down separate paths.

Michigan didn't want Penn State in the conference, and the school's stance fueled passions heading into the initial matchup. Beaver Stadium was pulsating when the Nittany Lions kicked off on a sunny afternoon in October 1993. But the excitement soon dissipated. Settling in under center, Michigan quarterback Todd Collins turned to an official claiming the team couldn't hear his signals. The play clock was turned off and Michigan tried again. Now the crowd was even louder. Collins again turned to the official, and the crowd received a warning. When Collins turned a third time after the crowd refused to hush, Penn State was penalized by losing a timeout. That did the trick. Collins took his place at the line and the Penn State–Michigan series was underway.

Whether Collins' stunt served any real purpose is still in dispute. Penn State fans remember it as a silly ploy unbecoming a school of Michigan's stature. Michigan fans just snicker. Which, of course, is their right. The Wolverines won that first game, 21–13. And except for a three-game stretch that included a thrilling 31–24 Penn State victory in the Big House in 1994, they and their fans have been chuckling ever since.

The most painful of Penn State's losses was undoubtedly the 2005 game. The unbeaten Nittany Lions held a 25–21 lead with 53 seconds remaining after Michael Robinson scored on a 3-yard keeper. But following a 41-yard kickoff return by Steve Breaston, Michigan maneuvered downfield. With the help of a controversial officiating decision in which two seconds were restored to the game clock at the insistence of Michigan Coach Lloyd Carr, quarterback Chad Henne threw a 10-yard pass to Mario Manningham on the final play of the game for a touchdown and a 27–25 victory.

It was the only loss of Penn State's season, and it was a heartbreaker. Paterno appeared ashen as he spoke to the press shortly after the game ended. He was asked where the Lions were headed. The question was intended metaphorically, but that's not how the coach took it. "I just want to get the players on the bus and get them home," he said. "It was a tough loss."

PENN STATE VS. NOTRE DAME

The rout was on. Notre Dame had a victory over Penn State in the bag. The Nittany Lions were looking fatigued on defense, sloppy on offense and were trailing the Fighting Irish by 24 points, 27–3, as the third quarter drew to a close. The only dilemma left for Notre Dame Coach Charlie Weis on this day was an ethical one. Should he keep pouring it on? Or should he give the Lions a reprieve with the outcome more or less decided? Such decisions always invite intro-spection. What's right? What's necessary? What would Touchdown Jesus do?

The Irish kept pouring it on. They faked a punt to set up a score. They continued passing with a 31-point lead and went for it on fourth-and-1 early in the fourth quarter to set up another touch-down. Final score: Notre Dame 41, Penn State 17. And as lopsided as it seemed, Notre Dame came away feeling that it really had called off the dogs. "I'm never one to try to score a hundred," Weis said. "That's not my deal. My deal is to

Penn State and Notre Dame have played a number of games with national implications.

win the football game and win it the right way."

Winning the right way. That's a familiar refrain when Penn State and Notre Dame play. The two schools are known for their tradition, their prestige, their high academic standards and occasionally their sanctimony. They graduate a lot of players, and yet they play important football games from time to time, the 2006 game being no exception. Weis had every reason to want a convincing victory over Penn State. His team went into the game ranked No. 4 and had hopes of playing for a national championship. That's not an uncommon concern in this rivalry.

Since first meeting in 1913, Penn State and Notre Dame have played a number of games with title implications. Penn State's road to the 1982 and 1986 national championships went through South Bend.

In 1982, the Lions defeated Notre Dame, 24–14. It was the team's first visit to Notre Dame Stadium since 1928, and players had stars in their eyes as they took in the scene, marveling at the Golden Dome and Touchdown Jesus. But once the game started, they were all business. Curt Warner rushed for 143 yards and the Irish, playing most of the game without injured quarterback Blair Kiel, weren't able to rally.

Penn State won again four years later, 24–19. The Irish were in their first season under Coach Lou Holtz and had been inconsistent in compiling a 4–4 record. Nevertheless, they threw a scare into Penn State. Steve Beuerlein passed for 311 yards but came up 13 yards short of an upset. In the final minute, Bob White sacked the senior quarterback for a 9-yard loss on second-and-goal, and the Irish

were unable to regroup. A third-down pass into the end zone fell incomplete and on fourth down, Mark Green slipped at the 13, giving the Lions possession and ending the threat.

Notre Dame turned the tables in 1998. Led by quarterback Tony Rice and nose tackle Chris Zorich, the Irish shut down Penn State, 21–3, en route to their 11th national championship. The season-ending loss was significant for Penn State, too. It left the Lions with a 5–6 record and saddled them with their first losing season since 1938.

The best of the high-stakes games between Penn State and Notre Dame was the one in which the favorite didn't prevail. The top-ranked Irish went into their 1990 home game against Penn State hoping to use it as a springboard to another national championship matchup. After taking leads of 14–0 and 21–7, they seemed poised to do just that.

But Penn State stormed back both times on the arm of junior quarterback Tony Sacca. With the score tied, 21–21, in the fourth quarter, Irish quarterback Rick Mirer overthrew a third-down pass and Darren Perry intercepted, returning the ball to the Notre Dame 19-yard line. Onto the field trotted true freshman kicker Craig Fayak. With four seconds left, Fayak sent the ball tumbling through the uprights from 34 yards away. Penn State had just pulled off the season's biggest upset.

"It's hard to describe the feeling," tailback Leroy Thompson told *The Pittsburgh Press*. "Everybody was hugging each other. There were guys crying. I was crying."

Back in State College, fans poured onto Beaver Avenue in a spontaneous outburst of joy. Pumping their fists, jabbing their fingers

Tony Hunt finds plenty of running room against the Irish in 2006.

into the air, they looked as though they were celebrating a national championship. They were not. Penn State, which went into the game with two losses, had already struck a deal to play in the Blockbuster Bowl.

But there's no underestimating the significance of a victory over Notre Dame, which leads the all-time series, 9–8–1. Regardless of whether there are titles on the line, these two teams can always find a reason to go after each other hard. It's the kind of rivalry that occurs between schools with so much in common.

Paterno was asked recently whether he was a Notre Dame fan growing up in Brooklyn in the 1930s and 1940s. After recounting his Catholic school upbringing, he began telling a story about his oldest son, David.

David Paterno had been thinking about where he wanted to attend college. His father kept trying to sell him on Notre Dame. The elder Paterno arranged a visit, but when David got to his hotel, he became ill and ended up spending the whole weekend in his room. He didn't end up in South Bend, and his father couldn't help but feel a bit disappointed.

"I would have liked to have seen one of my kids go," he said. "It's a great school with a great tradition. It's fun to go out there and play."

PENN STATE VS. MICHIGAN STATE

Of all the Nittany Lions' signature games, this one gets the least respect. Every November, these two historic programs square off. And every November, fans on both sides go through the motions, hoping to see some sparks fly but feeling, in the end, that it's just another game. Why the disdain? Because even though the Penn State-Michigan State series has the trappings of a great rivalry, there's something missing. These two teams just don't hate each other. In fact, they kind of like each other. What kind of rivalry is that?

Penn State's relationship with Michigan State dates back to 1914, when the school was still known as Michigan Agricultural College. The visiting Aggies won that initial meeting, 6–3. The Lions evened the series with a 13–6 victory in 1925, but Michigan State dominated the eight games between the two teams in the 1940s, 1950s and 1960s, going 7–0–1. The last of those matchups, a 1966 game in East Lansing, was the most painful for Penn State. Michigan State's All-America defensive end Bubba Smith blindsided Jack White in the second quarter, leaving the quarterback with a bleeding kidney. The Spartans went on to crush Penn State, 42–8. It was Paterno's first defeat as a head coach.

The rivalry went dormant after that game and didn't begin to revive until 1989, when a startling piece of news broke: the Big Ten was going to invite Penn State to join. Michigan State Coach George Perles was in Hawaii at the time getting his team ready for the Aloha Bowl. From the Spartans' practice field, he called Paterno to welcome him into the conference,

The Lions hold a slim 12–11–1 lead in their rivalry with Michigan State.

and to make a proposal. Perles wanted the schools to establish a rivalry game, to be played on the final day of the regular season. He thought it would be good for the two programs and good for the conference.

Paterno appreciated the offer. Officials at some other schools had expressed reservations about expanding the conference, but Michigan State supported Penn State's admission wholeheartedly. The Spartans knew what it felt like to be the new kid on the block. They were new kids themselves, at least by Big Ten standards, having joined in 1949.

And so a rivalry game was created. Officials promoted it as a natural outgrowth of Penn State's admission to the conference, noting the synchronicity of the schools' respective histories. Both were land-grant institutions and both were founded in 1855. Perles even helped design the trophy that was to go to the game's winner. It was called the Land Grant Trophy, and it looked like the kind of thing a football coach might design, blocky and thick with bits of statuary protruding from its brass-encrusted trunk.

Was that enough to get people's blood boiling the way it did when Michigan and Ohio State came to town? Do you even have to ask?

Penn State fans and Michigan State fans alike reacted with bewilderment. Rivalries weren't supposed to come prefabricated. They were supposed to be organic, developing slowly over the years as grudges and resentments accrued. As for the Land Grant Trophy, Penn State's Phil Ostrowski put it best during a news conference leading up to the 1997 game. Said the young offensive lineman, "There's a trophy?"

And yet there's an ironic edge to the criticism the rivalry has received. The truth is, the games themselves have been thrilling. Not all of them, maybe not even the majority of them. But the Spartans and Nittany Lions have played some entertaining football over the years including several games that have outshone Michigan-Ohio State, which is played on the same day.

The very first game in 1993 was a corker. Penn State trailed by 20 points late in the third quarter but stormed back and won, 38–37. Said Paterno, "This was the best comeback I can remember in a long time."

Two years later, the Lions pulled off another rally. Trailing by three, they had the ball at the Spartans' 4-yard line with 13 seconds remaining and no timeouts. The best course of action looked to be a pass into the end zone, but Penn State decided not to play it safe. Wally Richardson threw a screen pass to Bobby Engram at the 5, and the senior wideout lunged into the end zone to give the Lions a 24–20 victory.

In 1997, the Spartans dealt Penn State one of its most embarrassing defeats. Taking advantage of the fourth-ranked Lions' comically undersized defensive line, they sent Sedrick Irvin and Marc Renaud crashing through the middle and watched as both tailbacks surpassed 200 yards. Final score: Michigan State 49, Penn State 14. "They took it to us," said a dazed Penn State quarterback Mike McQueary.

The Nittany Lions got their revenge, and then some, by unleashing Larry Johnson on a hapless Spartans defense in 2002. Johnson needed 264 yards to become the first Big Ten running back to rush for 2,000 yards in a season. He got all he needed and more in the first half, bolting for 279 yards and four touchdowns in the first two quarters as the Lions romped, 61–7.

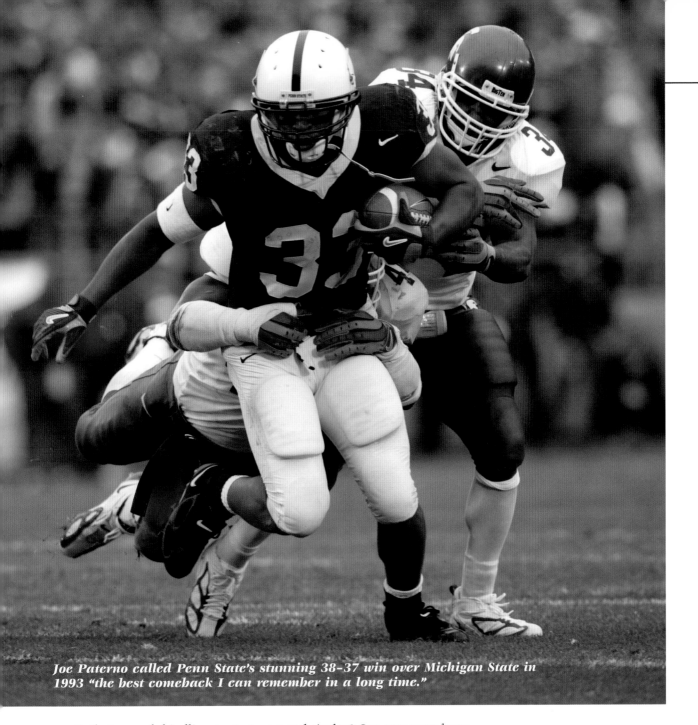

Joe Paterno called Penn State's stunning 38-37 win over Michigan State in 1993 "the best comeback I can remember in a long time."

Is that enough kindling to start up a real rivalry? Can you even have a real rivalry with an opponent that you admire? Yes, you can, Paterno believes. "When Perles called me, he was the first guy in the Big Ten to say, 'I'm glad you're in it. Why don't we establish some kind of relationship?' That really made me feel good. I thought it was a great idea. I still think it's a great idea."

PENN STATE VS. PITT

The year was 1893, and Penn State was eager to christen its new 500-seat football field, named for former Pennsylvania Govenor James Beaver. In those days, opponents made the difficult trek to State College reluctantly, if at all. As historian Lou Prato explains in his *Penn State Football Encyclopedia,* several teams turned down invitations to play Penn State in its new home. They wanted Penn State to come to them.

It fell to a team from the Western University of Pennsylvania to help inaugurate Beaver Field. The visitors could hardly have been more gracious. When heavy rain forced a two-day postponement, they happily extended their stay, agreeing to play on Monday rather than Saturday.

That team would eventually lose, 32–0, amid speculation that players had enjoyed a bit too much Penn State hospitality during their layover in State College. But even with the lopsided result, there was bonhomie in the air as the visitors departed. An account of the game, detailed by Prato, lauds WUP's sportsmanlike play, as exemplified by the "marked absence of slugging."

"Both teams behaved like gentlemen," the account continues. "We want the Western boys to come again and come often."

Who could have guessed?

Who could have guessed that Penn State and Pitt (as WUP later came to be known) would turn into the most bitter of rivals? That they would snipe at each other over Pitt's unwillingness to come back to Penn State on Joe Paterno's terms? That there would be plenty of slugging?

No rival in Penn State's long football history evokes more passion than Pitt. The teams have played each other infrequently since Penn State joined the Big Ten, but in western Pennsylvania it's as if the series never went away. Pitt fans reveled in the Nittany Lions' troubles of the early 2000s and crowed when Pitt won the most recent game between the teams, 12–0, at Three Rivers Stadium in 2000. Penn State fans returned fire when Penn State won the Orange Bowl in 2005 while Pitt was sitting at home after a 5–6 finish. So deep is this rivalry that it doesn't need to exist to get people's blood boiling.

Pitt and Penn State are archetypical enemies. They're the antagonists who hate each other because they're so much alike. Through the years, both teams have stocked up on players from the talent-rich Western Pennsylvania Interscholastic Athletic League, players who knew each other well and took their high school grudges with them to college. When the rivalry was at its peak, the players who shined brightest were the ones from western Pennsylvania. Pitt had Tony Dorsett and Dan Marino. Penn State countered with Bruce Clark, Greg Gattuso and Chuck Fusina.

The hostilities on the field occasionally spilled over into other areas. In his autobiography, Paterno recounted a story involving Pitt's Jackie Sherrill, one of the few coaches he openly disliked. According to Paterno, Sherrill became upset when he couldn't find a player that the two schools were recruiting and called Paterno's house well after midnight trying to find out where his rival coach was. Sue Paterno picked up the phone. "I know that son

The most bitter of all Penn State's rivals: the Pitt Panthers.

With the teams no longer meeting on an annual basis, Penn State's 50-42-4 lead in the series appears safe.

of a bitch has that kid, and I'm going to find him and beat the crap out of him," Sherrill told Paterno's wife according to the account in *Paterno: By the Book.* The incident only added to Paterno's disdain for Sherrill. "Brave, heroic man," he wrote sarcastically.

The two coaches have since patched things up, but in the late 1970s, tensions were running high. And with good reason. Back then, national championships were at stake when Penn State played Pitt. During a 10-year span from 1976 to 1985, there were four games in which one of those teams was ranked No. 1. There were two additional games in which both teams were ranked in the top five and one in which they were ranked in the top 10.

Pitt won the national championship in 1976 after defeating Penn State, 24–7, at Three Rivers Stadium. The Lions kept Dorsett in check in the first half, but the Panthers put their future Heisman Trophy winner at fullback in the second half and Penn State didn't know how to react. Dorsett finished with 224 yards as Pitt turned a 7–7 halftime deadlock into a comfortable victory.

The Lions won a championship of their own six years later and used a victory over Pitt as the springboard. Clamping down on the fifth-ranked Panthers' offense, the Lions prevailed, 19–10, and headed to the Sugar Bowl to face No. 1 Georgia.

The most memorable game of that era took place in 1981, when the Nittany Lions embarrassed the No. 1-ranked Panthers at home, 48–14. Pitt had taken on a 14–0 lead in the first quarter on the passing of Marino. But when Roger Jackson intercepted a pass in the end zone to thwart Pitt's next drive, the entire game changed. Penn State followed with six unanswered touchdowns and a couple of field goals. For Sherrill and the Panthers, it was a humbling experience. "I never dreamt this could happen," tight end John Brown told *The Pittsburgh Press.* "When it rains, it pours, and it really rained on us today."

Someone is always getting rained on in this rivalry. The Nittany Lions got off to a lousy start, losing 29 of the first 49 games between the schools. Most of those games were played in Pittsburgh, including 28 in a row from 1903 to 1930. Not until the 1960s would the series settle into something resembling a home-and-home pattern. Pitt supporters say the preponderance of home games in the early years of the rivalry was because Penn State wanted it that way. The Lions, they say, made more money playing in Pittsburgh because the Panthers had a bigger stadium. Penn State backers dispute that claim.

Regardless, there's no disputing that Paterno and his predecessor, Rip Engle, changed the balance of power when they arrived in State College in 1950. Engle went 9–6–1 against the Panthers, amassing more victories over the Lions' archrivals than his six predecessors put together. His protégé has done even better, going 23–7–1.

Some say Paterno has also gotten the better of Pitt in the schools' off-the-field jousting, which has always been a big part of the rivalry.

Most of these disputes can be traced back to Paterno's tenure as athletic director at Penn State, when he proposed an Eastern all-sports conference that would have banded together the Major Independents. Though well received by some Eastern schools, the proposal fell apart when Pitt joined the Big East in basketball. Paterno was deeply disappointed.

Pitt went on to enjoy great success in basketball thanks to its involvement in the fledgling Big East. Penn State, meanwhile, tried to build its basketball program via the Atlantic 10. The A-10 had only a fraction of the Big East's cache, and so Penn State maintained its interest in joining an all-sports conference. Eventually, that desire led school officials to began looking westward.

The rest is history.

As for the Penn State-Pitt series, well, that may be history, too.

The two teams have only played four times since 1992, with Penn State winning three of those games to run its record in the series to 50–42–4. Pitt has tried to rekindle interest in a home-and-home series but Paterno doesn't appear interested; his ground rules for any potential resumption would include an unbalanced schedule favoring Penn State. The talking points in this debate rarely change. Whenever the subject comes up, Paterno invariably cites the need for additional home football games so that Penn State can bankroll its nonrevenue teams. Pitt invariably balks, and the two sides go back to ignoring each other.

"You can't afford to have home and home with everybody," Paterno groused in 1997. "You need to every year plug in somebody who is willing to come to your place either two out of three times or come here every once in a while without you having to go back down and play at their home site. It's not an easy thing to do."

No kidding. The people may change, the circumstances may change, but some things seem destined to stay the same forever. More than a century after it all began, Penn State still wants those Western boys to come again and come often.

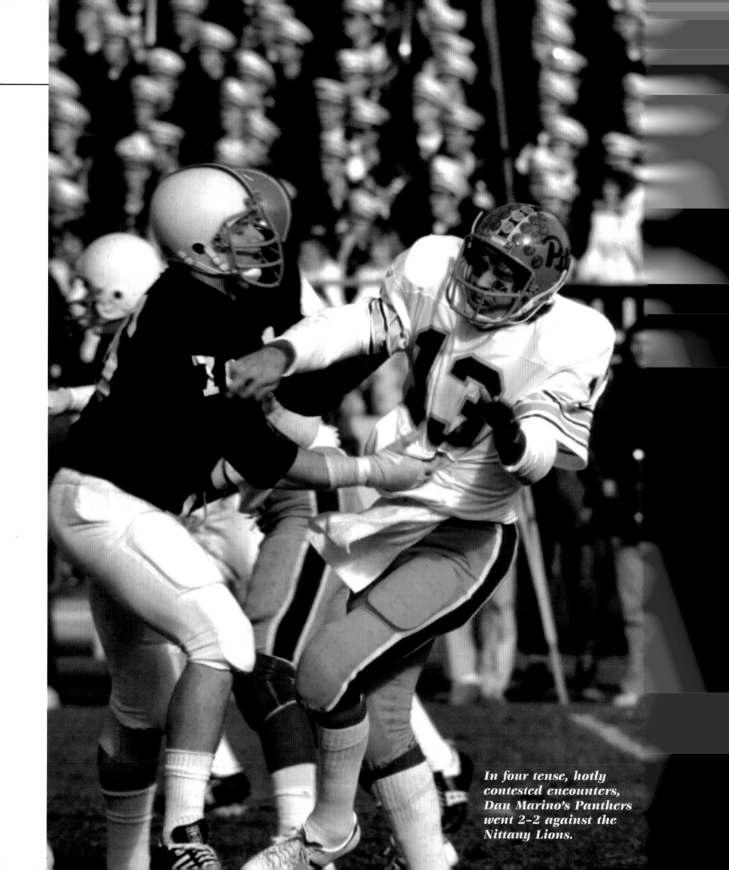

In four tense, hotly contested encounters, Dan Marino's Panthers went 2-2 against the Nittany Lions.

Paterno leads the team out of the tunnel.

Talkin' Penn State Football

We thought we'd go straight to the source and let some of Penn State's greatest legends share their thoughts about Nittany Lion football.

"My playing at Penn State made me better prepared for the pros in the sense of knowing the game. I learned a lot of stuff playing both defense and offense, and when I went to the Giants, I didn't feel like there was anyone I ever played against who was better than me."

—ROSEY GRIER, T, 1951–1954

"I've been told by a couple of people that Joe Paterno has called me the greatest football player ever to play for Penn State. That's an overwhelming statement, and I am truly humbled. When I'm told things like that, I wonder how can that be because there have been great ballplayers there for more than 100 years. I feel very honored just to be included in that group."

—LENNY MOORE, HB/KR, 1952–1955

"Being a Nittany Lion can be summed up in two words: *'plain'
and 'proud.' The plain aspect comes from basically a fairly conservative
approach to football. Nothing flashy. Very plain uniforms. The foundation for a lot of blue-collar football players. And from my experience,
first-generation college students. Plain people, yet very proud."*

—JERRY SANDUSKY, E, 1962–1965, AND LONGTIME ASSISTANT COACH,
DEFENSIVE COORDINATOR AND ARCHITECT OF "LINEBACKER U"

"It really didn't bother me *that we didn't win the national championship either of those two years [undefeated seasons in 1968 and 1969].
It's a much bigger deal today, being No. 1 in the country. I knew I'd
played on one of the best defenses in the country both those years, but
we had no control over the polls."*

—JACK HAM, LB, 1967–1970

"I said, 'Coach, I'm not interested in going to Penn State. *I'm
going to Ohio State.' He said to me, 'Well, you're afraid to come to Penn
State because Charlie Pittman is there and you can't play.' He ticked me
off a little bit, and within 10 seconds, I replied, 'I'm coming to Penn State
and I'm going to break all the records up there.' Even back then I think
Joe knew how to get to me and motivate me."*

—LYDELL MITCHELL, RB, 1968–1971

Lydell Mitchell

"You look back at [Joe Paterno] *and you look at what he's still doing and the sayings that he has and it's still the same. Don't get me wrong, every once in a while when you're out on the practice field and you're day to day with Joe, you want to go up and just grab him and want to shake him and say 'Hey, enough.' But you still find yourself hearing what he told you years ago and using the same sayings every once in a while."*

—HEISMAN WINNER JOHN CAPPELLETTI, TB/DB, 1970–1973

"I can still hear that strange voice *of his rippling across the practice field when he saw something he didn't like. He didn't play favorites. He'd throw me off the field as well as the next guy. You had to have thick skin. You knew there was a reason—it wasn't for lack of effort but he didn't like silly mistakes. I think the players felt a little bit better when he got in their face because we sort of knew there was a reason for it, that he expected more from us."*

—CHUCK FUSINA, QB, 1975–1978

"I had pro scouts tell me, 'You look at a Penn State kid *and you know exactly what you're going to get. You get a first-class kid. He's going to be respectful. He's going to be smart. He's going to work his tail off. He's not going to make mistakes. You know exactly what you're going to get. You know coming out of Penn State, out of Paterno, and out of the Penn State coaching staff that that's what you're going to get.' That's how everyone looks at Penn State. It's very positive, consistent, smart and classy. Being a Penn State football player carries instant respect and a positive reputation."*

—MATT SUHEY, TB/FB, 1976–1979

Matt Suhey

*"**I am very proud to have played football for Penn State** and especially proud and honored to have been the quarterback of Joe Paterno's first national championship team. Being a part of the Penn State football legacy is very special to me because I truly believe that we do it the right way. We win, we compete for championships, we graduate, and we display class and character on and off the field."*

— TODD BLACKLEDGE, QB, 1979–1982

*"**We heard 'How 'bout them Dawgs!'** over and over in the week leading up to the game. By the end of the week, we were determined to shut them up and shut them down."*

— CURT WARNER, RB, 1979–1982, ON THE SUGAR BOWL
WIN OVER GEORGIA THAT GAVE PENN STATE
THE NATIONAL CHAMPIONSHIP

*"**I was inducted into the Buffalo Hall of Fame,** and those people know me as a Buffalo Bill. My kids and people around Pittsburgh, which is big Penn State country and where I now live, know me as a Nittany Lion. I'll take that any day."*

— SHANE CONLAN, LB, 1982–1986

*"**In my mind, we're the greatest college football tradition that exists.**"*

— ANDRE COLLINS, LB, 1986–1989

"Joe came to me after the game and said, 'You did all you could for Penn State. Who am I to tell you to stay because I want you to stay? You can take care of your mom now.'"
—KI-JANA CARTER, RB, 1991–1994, ON PATERNO'S COUNSEL AFTER THE 1995 ROSE BOWL

"Joe Paterno always talked about pushing through obstacles and never giving up. Those are some of the things I remember about Joe and being at Penn State. It's hard to find another like him. He demanded a lot from his players, not just on the field but off the field, too. He had a standard about what a Penn State student-athlete is all about, and it goes for everybody."
—COURTNEY BROWN, DE, 1996–1999

"All we could do was win every game, and Joe wasn't in the business of running up the score. I just wish we would have had some way of settling it on the field like we saw USC and Texas do in the 2006 Rose Bowl. Then there would be no dispute."
—BOBBY ENGRAM, WR, 1991–1995, ON PENN STATE'S RUNNER-UP FINISH TO NEBRASKA IN THE FINAL POLLS AFTER THE 1994 SEASON DESPITE THEIR 12–0 RECORD

Joe Paterno

*"**I will never forget** when I was invited to the hospitality suite after the Orange Bowl. Someone asked Joe to have his picture taken with me and Franco Harris. Here I am standing next to Coach Paterno, one of the greatest coaches on any level of any sport ever, and Franco Harris, one of the legends of the NFL and of college, and they wanted me in the picture with them. It really meant a lot to me and really made me feel a sense of Penn State pride and a sense of accomplishment in my college career."*

—MICHAEL ROBINSON, QB, 2001–2005

*"**He's one of the best football players** we have had here at Penn State in the years I have been here. He is a great athlete and an outstanding leader, and he made a big difference in our [2005] season."*

—PATERNO ON ROBINSON

Michael Robinson

*"**You always hear the term 'Lion's Pride,'** and for me that really surfaced when the team struggled prior to 2005. No matter what, I always wear my Penn State stuff proudly. I used to go meetings with the Dolphins with my Penn State stuff on because I know what it means to be a Penn Stater. It's not about wins and losses. It's about what kind of man you develop into and how you go into the community and represent yourself and your family and university."*

—O.J. McDUFFIE, WR, 1988–1992

"To be honest with you, Penn State was my worst visit. *I was pretty much bored. But I liked it here because I wasn't coming here to party. I was really coming to go to school and play football. [Coach Paterno] had a plan for every player, to put in their minds that they wanted to come here and get an education, go to classes, be a good citizen and abide by all the rules he established."*

—TAMBA HALI, DE, 2002–2005

"What it means to be a Nittany Lion *is being a small part of something that's so big—part of a program that takes young kids from all different backgrounds and develops them into not only great football players but people who are going to be great fathers, great husbands, people who are going to have a positive impact on the world."*

—PAUL POSLUSZNY, LB, 2003–2006

"If we don't do our job and aren't successful, *it would almost be like down-grading the legacy. Those players brought all this tradition to Penn State, and we don't want to be the guys who are known for ruining that tradition. It's our job to make sure we carry it on."*

—POSLUSZNY, PRIOR TO THE 2006 SEASON

Paul Posluszny

"Those white uniforms are who we are. *Hardworking, regular people who play by the rules and do it the right way. And we are a team. We may be individuals, but we play as a team. The team comes first. There is one name on the uniforms. Penn State."*

—JOE PATERNO

Traditions and Pageantry

Penn State's football program is steeped in tradition, on the field and off. Some of the school's landmarks and rituals date back to the very first games played on campus. Here's a look.

THE NITTANY LIONS

To answer your first question: No, there is no such thing as a Nittany Lion. Never has been. Like unicorns, Bigfoot and the Loch Ness Monster, Penn State's distinctive mascot exists only in the imagination. It is not to be found in the wild, or anywhere else for that matter. It's been well over a century since lions of any kind roamed central Pennsylvania.

The Lions' nickname refers to Mount Nittany, the majestic 2,200-foot-high peak that overlooks the village of Lemont, just a few miles down the road from Penn State. The word "Nittany" comes from the Algonquian Indians. According to local legend, the mountain was formed by the Great Spirit in honor of the Indian princess Nita-Nee. Europeans later borrowed the term when they began settling the region in the 1700s.

The use of the word "Nittany" in connection with Penn State athletics dates to a baseball game against host Princeton in 1904. Shown a statue of Princeton's fearsome Bengal mascot, a Penn State player named Harrison D. Mason reportedly announced that the Nittany Mountain Lion was "the fiercest beast of them all." Penn State won the game, 8–1, and the nickname, concocted in a moment of inspired chicanery, took campus by storm. By 1907, the Nittany Lion was accepted as the school's mascot. The designation became official in 1942.

BLUE AND WHITE

Penn State's original colors were pink and black, as determined by a vote of the student body in 1887. The football team's first cheer went, "Wish, wack—pink black! P! S! C!" Fortunately, neither of these fledgling traditions lasted long.

Bleached by the elements, the pink stripes faded to white soon after their debut. Penn State students were unhappy with the resulting black-and-white color scheme and decided to substitute blue for black. The school, which was known as Pennsylvania State College before receiving university status in 1953, eventually adopted the new colors for its athletic teams.

As for the cheer, it remains a part of Penn State lore, if not an ongoing game day ritual. It used to appear on some athletic department press releases and was re-enacted by a group of about 150 students as part of the university's sesquicentennial celebration in 2004.

Attend a game today, however, and the loudest cheer you'll hear from fans is the famous "We are...Penn State!" call-and-response. Though a distinct improvement over its precursor, it's the most obvious cheer in all of college fandom. Really, if you're sitting in Beaver Stadium with a LaVar Arrington replica jersey on your back and a blue paw print on your cheek, who else would you be?

CAMPUS LANDMARKS

The Nittany Lion Shrine

Sculpted by Heinz Warneke in 1940, this iconic statue stands guard over Penn State's campus from its lair in front of a stand of trees in between Rec Hall and the Nittany Lion Inn. The Shrine has been a photo-op mainstay ever since it was dedicated in 1942. New graduates flock to it each May. Couples have their wedding photos taken there, and hordes of camera-wielding fans descend on the site on football game days, even though it sits on the opposite end of campus from Beaver Stadium. Some photos naturally have more impact than others. Penn State graduates of the mid-1980s will no doubt remember the "twins" poster, a dorm room favorite in which identical blondes posed astride the Lion wearing only their tear-away Penn State jerseys and their smiles.

The Shrine's fame has often made it a target. An ear was broken off once, requiring Warneke himself to replace it. But the most famous instance of vandalism involved Joe Paterno's wife, Sue. Hoping to incite student fury on the eve of a big game against Syracuse in 1966, she and some friends slathered the Lion in orange paint. It came off, but later that night, Syracuse fans did real damage by coating the Lion in an oil-based paint. Since then, Penn Staters have stood guard over the Lion on Homecoming weekend, though there vigils are now largely ceremonial.

The Creamery

Penn State had a creamery before it had a football team. This campus landmark produced its first batch of ice cream in 1865 and is now the largest university creamery in the country, consuming 4.5 million gallons of milk a year. About half of that total is supplied by a herd of 225 cows at the Dairy Production Research Center. This is, after all, an agricultural school.

The Creamery has long been a game day tradition for many Penn Staters, and it has become even more central to the school's tailgating culture now that it has moved to the ground floor of the new Food Science Building, just down the street from Beaver Stadium. One look at the Creamery's menu of 110 flavors is enough to dispel the myth that football and ice cream have nothing to do with one another. Amid the tubs of Alumni Swirl, Chips Ahoy and French Vanilla are two flavors that any Penn State fan should appreciate: Sandusky Blitz (banana-flavored ice cream with chocolate covered peanuts and caramel) and Peachy Paterno (peach-flavored ice cream with peach slices).

Beaver Stadium

Penn State's home field holds 107,282 spectators, making it the second-largest stadium in the country behind only Michigan Stadium. Despite its great capacity, it used to be notorious for having a lethargic atmosphere. It was the kind of place where older alumni would grumble about the price of hot dogs and yell at those in front of them to sit down.

But recent attempts to invigorate the crowd—efforts that have seen some of the Blue Band's traditional favorites supplanted by fusillades of throbbing electronica—have turned the once-peaceful stadium into an electrifying place to play. The past few seasons it has literally shaken with excitement, with fans hopping up and down whenever "Kernkraft 400" starts pulsing through the loudspeakers. The new atmosphere was a big part of the story when Penn State defeated Ohio State, 17–10, in 2005 to re-emerge onto the national stage after two consecutive losing seasons. "It's crazy," Penn State wide receiver Deon Butler said following the game. "It almost goes from dead silence to pure pandemonium."

Named in honor of James A. Beaver, a former Pennsylvania governor and early supporter of the school, Beaver Stadium first opened its gates in 1960. But its history goes back much further. It began as Beaver Field and was located on the opposite side of campus, adjacent to Rec Hall. Although parking was scarce, the location was in other ways ideal—too ideal as it turned out. School officials decided they needed the land for classrooms and evicted the football team in the late 1950s.

After the 1959 season, the field's 30,000 seats were broken down into 700 pieces and hauled to a site in the middle of an empty field a mile away. The new facility opened the following season with an additional 16,000 seats and was rechristened Beaver Stadium. Tailback Eddie Caye scored the first touchdown in stadium history in the first quarter of a 20–0 shutout of Boston College.

Beaver Stadium has undergone seven major revisions over the years. Taken together, these projects have more than doubled its size. The addition of an 11,500-seat upper deck above the south end zone in 2001 was the most controversial of all the expansions. The new seating areas obscured the view of Mount Nittany, a treasured part of the Beaver Stadium experience for many fans. But while some still grumble about the diminished view—not to mention the price of hot dogs—fans continue to fill this massive edifice on fall Saturdays.

THE BLUE BAND

The Blue Band is a Penn State institution. It has 300 members—252 instrumentalists, 32 silks, 14 majorettes, a featured twirler and a drum major. The drum major has one of the most crucial duties on game day. As part of the band's pregame performance, he struts out ahead of the band and performs a somersault, after which he salutes the crowd. According to superstition, this act is fraught with significance. A successful flip is said to foreshadow a victory. An unsuccessful flip—yes, he's been known to stumble upon landing—is much more ominous. It means the Lions will most likely lose.

Penn State's first band was a six-member drum and bugle corps formed in 1899. It became a brass band two years later after receiving a gift from philanthropist Andrew Carnegie. Instrumentalists wore military-style brown uniforms before switching to blue in 1923. Since then, the band has performed its repertoire of traditional crowd pleasers in 32 bowl games. It marched in the Bicentennial Constitution Celebration Parade in Philadelphia in 1987 and appeared in the Tournament of Roses Parade in 1995. Its renditions of John Philip Sousa marches and classic rock warhorses like "Pinball Wizard" and "Live and Let Die" will no doubt waft through Beaver Stadium for decades to come.

THE PENN STATE ALMA MATER

For the glory of old State,
For her founders strong and great,
For the future that we wait,
Raise the song, raise the song.

Sing our love and loyalty,
Sing our hopes that, bright and free,
Rest, O Mother dear, with thee,
All with thee, all with thee.

When we stood at childhood's gate,
Shapeless in the hands of fate,
Thou didst mold us, dear old State,
Dear old State, dear old State.

May no act of ours bring shame,
To one heart that loves thy name,
May our lives but swell thy fame,
Dear old State, dear old State.

MASCOT

At first glance, Penn State's costumed Nittany Lion mascot appears nondescript. He doesn't have Purdue Pete's hammer or Bucky Badger's overstuffed head, or Sparty's steroidal musculature. He's just a guy in a furry suit.

But once he starts to limber up, his appeal becomes clear. The Nittany Lion doesn't just stand around in the end zone and cavort with cheerleaders; he dances, he works out, he moves. At any moment, the Nittany Lion is apt to break into a rendition of "Thriller," complete with synchronized dancers and moves swiped from the Michael Jackson video. Or maybe he'll don his fat-Elvis jumpsuit and regale the crowd with some Las Vegas schmaltz. Or do some Rocky-style one-armed push-ups. He is, after all, duty bound to perform one such push-up for every point the Lions score.

The Nittany Lion mascot has been bringing joy to young Penn State fans since 1921. That's when a student named Richard Hoffman donned the first costume.

The original Lion costume looked a little different than the one in use today. It had the bushy mane and exaggerated facial features of an African lion. Those features grew smaller in later years and the mane disappeared altogether as the mascot took on the appearance of a North American forest cat. But even though its likeness has changed, the Lion is as iconic as ever. Whether dashing off another round of push-ups, or body surfing through a crowd of spectators, he is one of the most beloved institutions in all of Penn State lore.

TAILGATING

Penn State didn't invent tailgating, but
Nittany Lion football fans have embraced it
as passionately as any in the country. On
every football weekend, RVs begin stream-
ing into town on Friday afternoon. By
Saturday morning, the spacious lots around
Beaver Stadium are filled, the beer is on ice
and the scent of burgers and hot dogs is
carried on the wind across campus from a
thousand portable grills.

   University officials anticipated the tailgating phenomenon when they decided to
move the stadium to its present location.
They thought that the site's rolling hills and
lush grass would encourage picnickers to
attend football games. These days, much of
the grass has been replaced by asphalt, and
the lots are more congested with other athletic facilities having arisen in the shadow of
Beaver Stadium. But if the sights, sounds and
smells are any indication, the impulse to
turn every Penn State game into a party is as
strong as ever.

Facts and Figures

CAREER STATISTICAL LEADERS

- Rushes: 649, Curt Warner, 1979–1982
- Rushing Yards: 3,398, Curt Warner, 1979–1982
- Passing Attempts: 1,082, Zack Mills, 2001–2004
- Completions: 606, Zack Mills, 2001–2004
- Passing Yardage: 7,212, Zack Mills, 2001–2004
- Completion Percentage: 56.3, Kerry Collins, 1991–1994
- Touchdown Passes: 41, Todd Blackledge, 1980-82; Tony Sacca, 1988-91; Zack Mills, 2001–2004
- Receptions: 167, Bobby Engram, 1991, 1993–1995
- Receiving Yardage: 3,026, Bobby Engram, 1991, 1993–1995
- Receiving Touchdowns: 31, Bobby Engram, 1991, 1993–1995
- Total Offense: 7,796, Zack Mills, 2001–2004
- Punt Return Average: 17.6, Ron Younker, 1953–1954
- Kickoff Return Average: 29.6, Larry Joe, 1946–1948
- All-Purpose Yardage: 5,045, Larry Johnson, 1999-2002
- Punting Average: 43.0, George Reynolds, 1980–1983
- Scoring: 282, Craig Fayak, 1990–1993
- Interceptions: 19, Neal Smith, 1967–1969
- Tackles: 372, Paul Posluszny, 2003–2006
- Sacks: 33, Courtney Brown, 1996–1999
- Tackles for Loss: 70, Courtney Brown, 1996–1999

ALL-TIME BOWL GAME SCORES

Bowl	Date	Result
Rose	January 1, 1923	Southern Cal 14, Penn State 3
Cotton	January 1, 1948	Penn State 13, Southern Methodist 13
Liberty	December 19, 1959	Penn State 7, Alabama 0
Liberty	December 17, 1960	Penn State 41, Oregon 12
Gator	December 30, 1961	Penn State 30, Georgia Tech 15
Gator	December 29, 1962	Florida 17, Penn State 7
Gator	December 30, 1967	Penn State 17, Florida State 17
Orange	January 1, 1969	Penn State 15, Kansas 14
Orange	January 1, 1970	Penn State 10, Missouri 3
Cotton	January 1, 1972	Penn State 30, Texas 6
Sugar	December 31, 1972	Oklahoma 14, Penn State 0
Orange	January 1, 1974	Penn State 16, LSU 9
Cotton	January 1, 1975	Penn State 41, Baylor 20
Sugar	December 31, 1975	Alabama 13, Penn State 6
Gator	December 27, 1976	Notre Dame 20, Penn State 9
Fiesta	December 25, 1977	Penn State 42, Arizona State 30
Sugar	January 1, 1979	Alabama 14, Penn State 7
Liberty	December 22, 1979	Penn State 9, Tulane 6
Fiesta	December 26, 1980	Penn State 31, Ohio State 19
Fiesta	January 1, 1982	Penn State 26, Southern Cal 10
Sugar	January 1, 1983	Penn State 27, Georgia 23
Aloha	December 26, 1983	Penn State 13, Washington 10
Orange	January 1, 1986	Oklahoma 25, Penn State 10
Fiesta	January 2, 1987	Penn State 14, Miami (Florida) 10
Citrus	January 1, 1988	Clemson 35, Penn State 10
Holiday	December 29, 1989	Penn State 50, Brigham Young 39
Blockbuster	December 28, 1990	Florida State 24, Penn State 17
Fiesta	January 1, 1992	Penn State 42, Tennessee 17
Blockbuster	January 1, 1993	Stanford 24, Penn State 3
Citrus	January 1, 1994	Penn State 31, Tennessee 13
Rose	January 2, 1995	Penn State 38, Oregon 20
Outback	January 1, 1996	Penn State 43, Auburn 14
Fiesta	January 1, 1997	Penn State 38, Texas 15
Citrus	January 1, 1998	Florida 21, Penn State 6
Outback	January 1, 1999	Penn State 26, Kentucky 14
Alamo	December 28, 1999	Penn State 24, Texas A&M 0
Capital One	January 1, 2003	Auburn 13, Penn State 9
Orange	January 3, 2006	Penn State 26, Florida State 23
Outback	January 1, 2007	Penn State 20, Tennessee 10

Overall

Won 25, Lost 12, Tied 2

NITTANY LIONS IN THE COLLEGE FOOTBALL HALL OF FAME

Name	Position	Years	Inducted
Hugo Bezdek	Coach	1918–1929	1954
John Cappelletti	Halfback	1971–1973	1993
Keith Dorney	Offensive Tackle	1975–1978	2005
Rip Engle	Coach	1950–1965	1973
Jack Ham	Linebacker	1968–1970	1990
Dick Harlow	Coach	1915–1917	1954
Bob Higgins	Coach	1930–1948	1954
Glenn Killinger	Quarterback	1918–1921	1971
Ted Kwalick	Tight End	1966–1968	1989
Richie Lucas	Quarterback	1957–1959	1986
Pete Mauthe	Halfback	1909–1912	1957
Shorty Miller	Quarterback	1910–1913	1974
Lydell Mitchell	Running Back	1969–1971	2004
Dennis Onkotz	Linebacker	1967–1969	1995
Mike Reid	Defensive Tackle	1966, 1968–1969	1987
Glenn Ressler	Center/Guard	1962–1964	2001
Dave Robinson	End	1960–1962	1997
Steve Suhey	Guard	1942, 1946–1947	1985
Dexter Very	End	1909–1912	1976
Harry Wilson	Halfback	1921–1927	1973

NITTANY LIONS IN THE PRO FOOTBALL HALL OF FAME

Jack Ham, LB
Inducted 1988
Penn State, 1968–1970
Pittsburgh Steelers, 1971–1982
• Played on four Super Bowl–winning teams
• All-Pro nine consecutive seasons
• NFL Team of the Decade for the 1970s
• 32 career interceptions

Franco Harris, FB
Inducted 1990
Penn State, 1969–1971
Pittsburgh Steelers, 1972–1983
Seattle Seahawks, 1984
• Rushed for 12,120 yards and scored 91 touchdowns
• Topped the 1,000-yard mark eight times
• MVP of Super Bowl IX
• Played in nine Pro Bowls

August Michalske, G
Inducted 1964
Penn State, 1923–1925
New York Yankees (AFL), 1926
New York Yankees (NFL), 1927–1928
Green Bay Packers, 1929–1935, 1937
• Member of three NFL Championship teams in Green Bay (1929–1931)
• Outstanding lead guard, feared defender whose blitzing technique was ahead of its time

Lenny Moore, RB
Inducted 1975
Penn State, 1953–1955
Baltimore Colts, 1956–1967
• Five-time All-Pro
• Scored a touchdown in a record 18 consecutive games
• 12,451 career combined yards
• 113 career touchdowns

Mike Munchak, G
Inducted 2001
Penn State, 1979–1981
Houston Oilers, 1982–1993
• Nine-time Pro Bowler
• Centerpiece of offensive line that helped Oilers to seven consecutive playoff appearances
• Played in 159 regular-season games

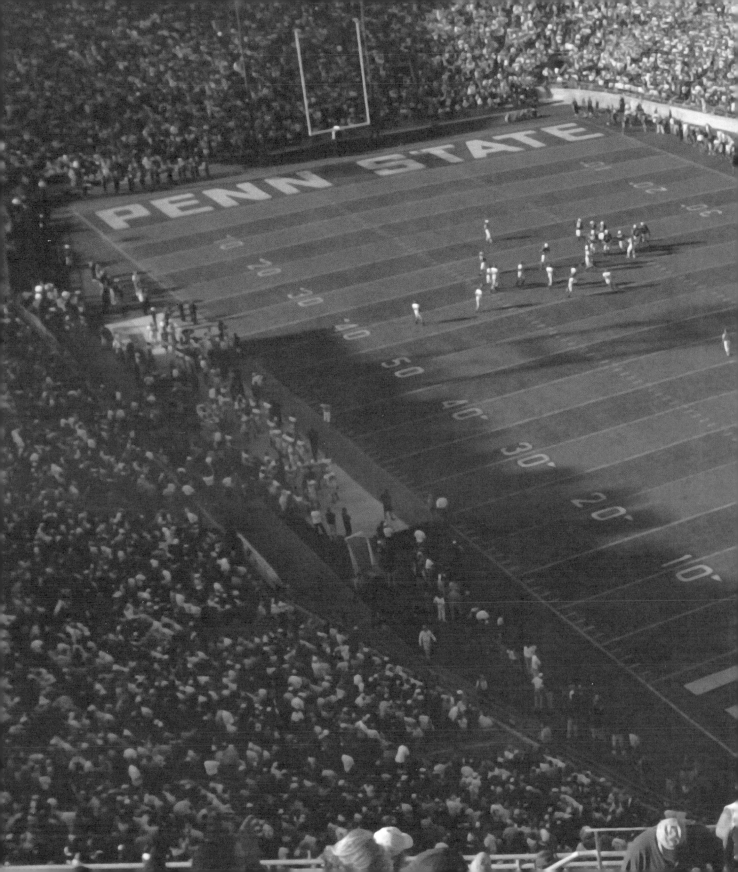